·THE HAND TOOL COMPANION·

**Other Books by
Katie and Gene Hamilton**

Don't Move, Improve!

Fix It Fast, Fix It Right

How to Be Your Own Contractor

Quick Fix Home Repair Handbook

Wooden Toys

Build It Together

Keep It Working . . . Longer, Better!

· THE ·
HAND TOOL
COMPANION

The Back-to-Basics Guide
for Learning About and
Using Hand Tools

Katie and Gene Hamilton

An Owl Book

HENRY HOLT AND COMPANY
NEW YORK

Henry Holt and Company, Inc.
Publishers since 1866
115 West 18th Street
New York, New York 10011

Henry Holt® is a registered
trademark of Henry Holt and Company, Inc.

Copyright © 1994 by Katie and Gene Hamilton
All rights reserved.
Published in Canada by Fitzhenry & Whiteside Ltd.,
195 Allstate Parkway, Markham, Ontario L3R 4T8.

Library of Congress Cataloging-in-Publication Data
Hamilton, Katie.
The hand tool companion: the back-to-basics guide for learning
about and using hand tools / Katie and Gene Hamilton.—1st ed.
p. cm.
"An Owl book."
1. Tools. I. Hamilton, Gene. II. Title.
TJ1195.H13   1994   93-39823
621.9'08—dc20   CIP

ISBN 0-8050-2498-0

Henry Holt books are available for special promotions
and premiums. For details contact:
Director, Special Markets.

First Edition—1994

DESIGNED BY LUCY ALBANESE
ILLUSTRATED BY LAURA HARTMAN MAESTRO

Printed in the United States of America
All first editions are printed on acid-free paper. ∞

1   3   5   7   9   10   8   6   4   2

· CONTENTS ·

PART III: WOODWORKING PROJECTS

• ACKNOWLEDGMENTS •

We dedicate this book to our readers with the hope that they'll enjoy working with hand tools and encourage others to pick up a chisel or plane and create something meaningful for themselves and their families.

We'd like to thank our editor, Jo Ann Haun, for her enthusiasm and guidance; Laura Hartman Maestro, whose fine art illustrates the book; and our agent, Jane Jordan Browne, who has supported our efforts for so many years.

· THE HAND TOOL COMPANION ·

• Introduction •

Hand tools were an integral part of the lives of the early settlers in our country. They were used day after day to build furniture, cabins, and barns, and to mend tables, fences, and horse carriages. In those times a well-used hand tool was treasured like an heirloom quilt or a family Bible and was passed down from one generation to another.

Today the simplicity of hand tools has captured the spirit of a growing number of people who enjoy working with their hands and who want to experience the undeniable sense of accomplishment that comes with successfully completing a project. For some it's the desire to get back to basics and simplify the way they do things. For others there's a romantic element of being one with natural materials and working with care and precision to create something of value.

Our goal for this book is to combine the romance of using hand tools with the practical needs of being a homeowner. We think hand tools offer a viable alternative to using power tools for several reasons. Hand tools are inexpensive and their compact size makes them convenient to store just about anywhere. They are easy to maintain, requiring only a small amount of upkeep, and they can provide a lifetime of service.

Then there's the pleasing side effects of working with hand tools—the smell of fresh wood shavings as they fall to the floor and the near silence as the tool moves through the wood. And there's an undeniable sense of independence as knowing hands guide a well-honed tool to create and shape wood.

Part I is a primer on hand tools explaining what they do and how to use them. Part II takes you through the steps of seven home repair and improvement projects. Part III has seventeen projects to build for inside and outside your house.

We hope this book encourages you to use hand tools to make repairs and improvements around your house and to build projects with them that will enhance your spirit as well as your home.

A WORD ABOUT SAFETY
AND HAND TOOLS

In Part I we'll describe each tool and show how to use it properly. In general, however, there are a few words to be said about safety in using hand tools. Keep the blades, tips, and other cutting surfaces sharpened so you don't overwork or force a tool, causing it to bind or buckle under pressure. Use the tool the way it was designed to be used; don't use a chisel as a screwdriver or a vise to hold more than its capacity. Store hand tools in a drawer or box so they are always accessible and cannot get tangled up with cords or banged against other tools.

SHOPPING FOR LUMBER

Lumber is categorized in three grades: clear, common, and construction. You can expect clear lumber to be free of knots and twists and to cost the most. Common-grade lumber has some knots and surface blemishes but will be better-looking than the least expensive construction grade, which is used by carpenters for rough framing work. A piece of wood is considered lumber if it is 2 to 5 inches thick, and it is called a board if it is less than 2 inches thick.

When you look at a board or piece of lumber there are three parts. It has front and back faces, which are its widest surfaces, two edges on the sides, and two ends where it has been cut off. Notice the rough end grain on both ends, which shows the composition of the wood.

When you buy lumber you'll see that it is sold stacked together in bundles or standing loosely in bins marked by size. Lumber has a nominal size and actual size. A one-by-four is named for its nominal size, but its actual measurements are ¾ inch by 3½ inches. It is sold in various lengths up to 14 feet.

Most of the readily available lumber sold in yards and home centers is soft wood such as pine and fir. Hardwoods such as oak, mahogany, and walnut are sold by specialty woodworking suppliers, which you'll find listed in the yellow pages under "Woodworking."

MAIL-ORDER SOURCES

Klockit
P.O. Box 636
Lake Geneva, Wisconsin 53147
(800) 556-2548

Woodcraft
210 Wood Country Industry Park
P.O. Box 1686
Parkersburg, West Virginia 26102-1686
(800) 225-1153

The Woodworkers' Store
21801 Industrial Blvd.
Rogers, Minnesota 55374-9514
(800) 279-4441

•PART ONE•

Tools

Here's a look at the common and woodworking hand tools that we use for the projects in this book. They are basic tools that form the foundation of a well-rounded collection and will take you through most home repair and woodworking projects. There are, of course, a host of single-purpose specialty tools with specific functions for particular jobs. Depending on the type of work you enjoy you may want to collect some of these specialty tools over the years to add to your tool chest.

Buy the most expensive tool you can afford with an eye toward quality and craftsmanship. A hand tool is a good investment because you'll find yourself using it for mending and building projects around the house for years to come.

If you're like us you'll find other uses for your hand tools, too. We have a special stash of "boat tools" that we keep on board for fixing and maintaining our sailboat. We have another small bag of hand tools for repairing our bicycles that we take on rides in case we have a

breakdown or need to make a roadside repair. Because they are small, easy to transport, and don't require electricity or batteries to operate, hand tools can be used just about anywhere. An illustration of each tool appears following its description below.

Common Hand Tools

An **adjustable wrench** has jaws that can be opened or closed with a thumbscrew. Its movable jaws allow the wrench to fit nuts and bolts of differing diameters. This tool comes in various sizes, but the 10-inch size will fit most nuts and bolts found around the house.

The **carpenter's level** is a wooden or metal bar approximately 3 inches high by 24 inches long with liquid-filled glass or plastic vials, each containing a bubble that, when centered, indicates true vertical or horizontal. A carpenter's level is essential when you're building projects that must be straight and true. It is also helpful when you're laying out wallpaper and ceramic tile and for installing things like shelving or hanging pictures.

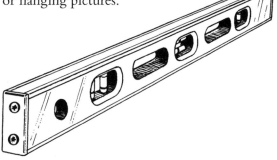

C-clamps are the most popular type of clamps. They are shaped like an angular C and made of cast iron with an adjustable screw on one end. They are used to hold surfaces together while you work on them. They come in various sizes up to 12 inches.

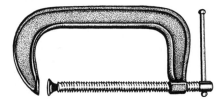

The **claw hammer** is the most common type of hammer. It has a metal head with a flat striking surface on one end and a notched claw used for removing nails from wood on the other. It is used for driving nails into wood and other surfaces. A 16-ounce hammer is the most useful for general hammering around the house.

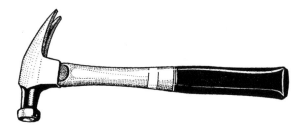

A **chalk line** is a handheld metal reel with a coiled string contained in a housing that holds a supply of powdered chalk. To use, pull the string out of the chalk line body and stretch it tightly between two marks. Then pluck the string to transfer chalk from the string onto the surface, creating a straight line.

A **combination square** is a steel ruler with a movable slide that has one face made perpendicular to the ruler and the other at a 45-degree angle. It is used to mark boards for cutting and to check the squareness of cuts. The ruler can also be used as a depth gauge or to lay out marks in the center of boards. Most combination squares come with a small spirit level in the movable head and a steel scribe for marking wood. No toolbox should be without this tool.

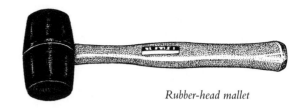
Rubber-head mallet

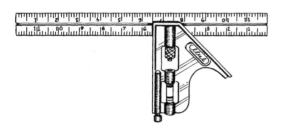

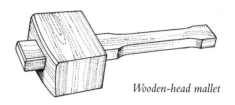
Wooden-head mallet

The **hacksaw** is a rigid saw with a removable, fine-toothed blade designed to cut metal. The hacksaw can also cut plumbing pipes, plastic, metal, and ceramic tile. The frame holds a thin blade that can be rotated to cut in various directions. The blades are inexpensive and should be changed as soon as they appear dull.

A **nail set** is a small metal shaft with one end pointed and the other end blunt. It is used with a hammer to "set" the nail, or drive the nail head below the surface of wood to conceal the nail.

Slip-joint pliers have adjustable jaws and are used for gripping and holding an object.

A **mallet** is a soft-headed hammer to be used whenever a claw hammer will damage the surface of what you are striking. The head is usually made of rubber or wood, and the handle is wooden. This tool is also used to drive chisels and other wooden-handled tools.

A **pry bar** is a flat steel bar with beveled edges in its ends and a hole in one end that can be used to pull nails from wood. Pry bars are also used to remove molding from walls or to separate wood that is nailed together. Its configuration is designed to provide leverage when forcing things apart. A small pry bar is a handy tool, especially for house repairs.

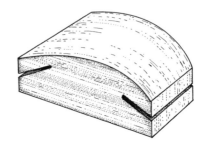

A **standard screwdriver** has a steel shaft with a flat blade and fits a standard straight slot.

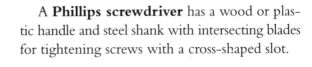

A **putty knife** is a flexible-bladed knife with a 1-inch or wider metal blade. It is used to apply spackling compound and to scrape surfaces.

A **Phillips screwdriver** has a wood or plastic handle and steel shank with intersecting blades for tightening screws with a cross-shaped slot.

A **tape measure** (also called a tape rule) is a flexible steel rule marked in inches and feet used to measure distances.

A **sanding block** is a rubber holder with a flat face, designed to fit a half-sheet of sandpaper. It can also be a palm-size block of wood wrapped with sandpaper. Either is useful because the hard, flat surface delivers a much more even sanding job than does sandpaper alone.

A **try square** is an L-shaped tool with a wooden handle and metal measuring blade used to test for the squareness of surfaces that are joined together.

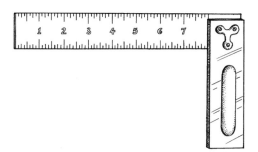

A **utility knife** is an all-purpose tool for cutting string, opening packing cartons, and trimming screening fabric, wallcoverings, and drywall. It has a metal handle with a compartment for storing blades and an open-and-close mechanism that slides a blade out for use and back into reserve when it is no longer needed.

Woodworking Hand Tools
DRILLING TOOLS

Brace and Bit

A brace is a tool that makes holes in wood. At one end an opening, or chuck, holds various sizes of auger bits, ranging from ¼ inch to 2 inches, depending on the size of the hole needed. The other end is the head, with a knob that you grip to operate the tool. In the middle there's a crank handle that you turn to drive the bit into the surface of the wood. It has a ratchet that gives you leverage so you can turn it both ways, maximizing your turning stroke.

You'll find many uses for this hand tool—whenever there's a need to make a hole larger than ¼ inch in diameter. For example, when installing a door lock, the opening for the latch mechanism requires a round hole. So does running pipe through floor joists in the basement or cable wires through rafters in the attic. If you are boring holes for bolts of any size, a brace and bit makes short work of the task. When operating, hold the brace straight so the hole will be properly aligned and not slanted. Hold the knob firmly and line up the chuck directly above the hole being drilled.

To maintain a brace periodically add a drop of oil to its two oil ports. One is located in the upper handle and the other is on the ratchet mechanism.

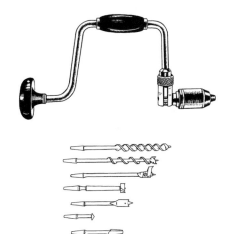

Hand Drill

A hand drill makes small holes in wood. The tool looks like an eggbeater and operates under the same principle. As you turn the cranklike handle, the gears rotate, controlling the drill bit in the chuck. As you rotate the crank clockwise the bit drills into the wood; when you do it backward or counterclockwise the drill bit backs out.

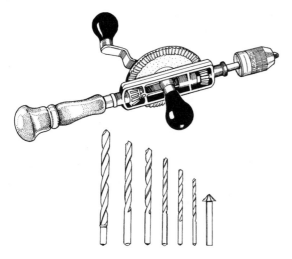

To insert a bit into the chuck, open its jaws by turning it so the opening is wide enough to hold the drill bit shaft. Hold the drill by the body with one hand to keep the handle from turning and with your other hand twist the chuck, tightening it around the bit.

You'll find sets of drill bits with a wide range of diameters to give you a variety of hole sizes. Holes over ¼ inch in diameter are better made with a brace and bit.

You'll use this tool whenever you're making small holes such as pilot holes for nails or screws for a woodworking project.

To drill straight holes, begin by marking the point with a nail set and hammer to make a depression in the wood. Hold the hand drill in a vertical position and grip it firmly as you turn the crank. If you're unsure of yourself, practice on a piece of scrap wood to become familiar with operating the drill.

If you don't want to drill completely through a piece of wood or want to make a series of holes the same depth, place a piece of tape around the drill bit at the depth you want the drill to go into the wood. The tape will warn you when you have reached the desired depth.

Chisels

A chisel looks something like a screwdriver, with a sturdy handle and a wide, sharp-edged, beveled blade. But it is not used like a screwdriver at all. Instead, a chisel is designed to chip away pieces of wood either alone or with a mallet tamping on the end of the handle to nudge it through the wood. Furniture makers use a chisel for cutting a mortise or for shaving off excess wood in a groove. Homeowners will want to use a chisel whenever it's necessary to carefully remove wood. In a remodeling project, when a board requires notching or the last piece of decking needs to be shaved to fit in place, a chisel is the tool to use.

There are a number of specialty chisels used by boat builders, cabinetmakers, and carvers that range from ⅛ inch to 2 inches wide with plastic, wooden, and steel handles. A good choice for the homeowner is a set of ¼-, ½-, ¾-, and 1-inch chisels with plastic handles, which

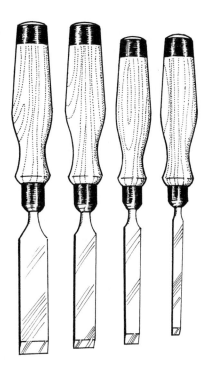

should cover most repairs and woodworking projects.

You can use a chisel with the bevel side up or down, depending on the task at hand. Use it with the bevel side down when you're removing wood or smoothing a surface. Use it with the bevel side up when you're flattening an area like the bottom of a hinge mortise and when you're cutting into the side of a board. Hold the chisel in one hand and place the other hand at the top of the blade to apply pressure and guide it through the wood. Use your thumb or forefingers to gently press down on the chisel as it works its way through the wood.

Use a clamp or vise to secure the wood and give yourself plenty of room around it. Move the wood so that you're working the chisel in an upward motion with the wood grain. Keep the chisel nearly flat against the surface as you advance the chisel through the wood in short smooth strokes.

CLAMPS

Bar Clamp

This all-purpose clamp has two clamping jaws joined by a steel beam or bar. One jaw has a screw-type clamp in it and is fixed to the end of the bar; the other slides up and down the bar and is held in position by a locking cam or disk clutch.

Bar clamps are adjustable and can be used to hold objects from ½ foot to about 3 feet wide. A bar clamp is a handy device for holding glued-up pieces of wood together while they dry, such as a mended chair leg or pieces of a woodworking project. To operate a bar clamp, back off the clamping screw until its head is resting on the fixed jaw. Then slide the movable jaw down the bar far enough to allow you to place the wood you want to clamp between the jaws. Then slide the movable end against the wood and lock the clutch. To tighten the clamp, turn the screw at the fixed end to apply enough pressure to hold the object firmly in position. To release the clamp, back off the screw and release the movable jaw.

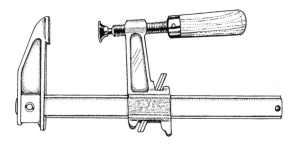

Pipe Clamp

These heavy-duty clamps work on the same principal as the bar clamp but use a pipe to connect the jaws. Pipe clamps come in kits that include only the jaw assemblies; you supply the pipe. They come in two sizes to fit ½-inch or ¾-inch pipe. The reach of these clamps is limited only by the length of the pipe.

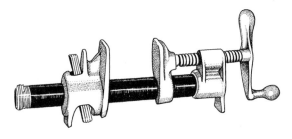

Web Clamp

This tool consists of a 12- to 15-foot length of 1-inch wide nylon web attached to a ratchet mechanism. This ratchet tightens the belt, applying even pressure to all sides of the object. A web belt is useful when clamping an odd-sized object such as the back of a chair or a picture frame. It is particularly useful when clamping an object with a delicate finish because the soft webbing material doesn't damage it.

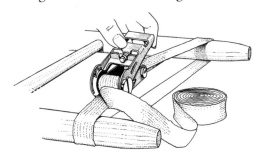

FILES AND RASPS

These tools are mainstays in any homeowner's toolbox. A file can be used on wood or metal, while a rasp is used only on wood. The working surface of a file or a rasp has teeth that cut into any kind of wood that requires smoothing and shaping, even tough end grain.

The tools are long steel rods or bars with one smooth end, called the tang, which is used as a handle. For more control and to protect your hands you can buy a wooden handle that fits onto a file or a rasp and makes handling it easier. Think of using a file or rasp as you would a heavy-duty emery board, working it back and forth over a surface to smooth and shape it.

A file used to scrape wood has single cut-teeth running in parallel diagonal lines or double-cut teeth that have a second set of teeth running diagonally across the first. A 10-inch double-cut and a 4-inch triangular file are good all-purpose files for completing repair jobs around the house. The larger flat file will shape framing lumber and remove material from holes and openings, and the smaller triangular file will fit into tight spots to remove wood from where it's not wanted.

Use a file to maintain tools by sharpening scrapers, saws, and screwdrivers with it. Sharpen the sides of shovels and garden tools too so their steel sides dig deep and sharp into the ground.

When using a file on a piece of lumber, put the object being worked on in a vise or secure it to something so it cannot move. The piece being worked on should be near elbow height.

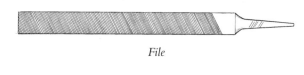

File

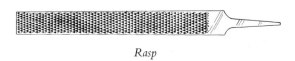

Rasp

For delicate work, raise the work to eye level and wear safety goggles.

You work a file in two ways. Begin by rough cutting, or working the file at an angle, pressing firmly down against the surface going in one direction. Applying downward pressure is important to prevent "chattering," or skipping over the surface, which gives you uneven results. With the file in both hands, push it across the work and then lift it up. Continue cross filing until the surface has changed to your satisfaction. Then move the piece being worked on (or reposition yourself) so you can push the file at right angles in the same one-stroke method to further smooth out the surface.

While a file scrapes wood, a rasp takes the wood off in bites or chunks, so a light sanding is often needed after shaping wood with a rasp. It cuts rougher but faster than a file so be careful that you don't take more surface off than you intend when using it. Use it in the same way as the file, holding it firmly as you push it across the wood. An 8-inch half-round rasp is a handy tool to have because it can do everything from rough cutting the curves on a woodworking project to chewing out predrilled holes in a swing set you're trying to assemble.

MARKING GAUGE

This handheld tool looks like a short measuring rod running through a small block of wood. The rod is held in place with a thumbscrew so it is adjustable. A marking pin located in the end of the rod scribes the wood as the tool is run across it. It is used to mark off guidelines for woodworking.

To operate the gauge loosen the thumbscrew and slide the rod through the block until the marking pin is positioned the desired distance from the block. Then tighten the thumbscrew to secure it. To mark the wood, hold the block against the edge of the board and pull the gauge along the board, putting pressure on the pin with your other hand.

A marking gauge is useful when setting out a row of holes for drilling or for lining up a cut-line in a woodworking project.

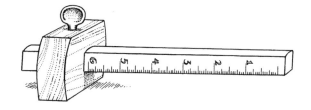

MITER BOX

A wooden miter box is used to make precise 45-degree or 90-degree cuts in wood such as for corner molding edges and picture frames. It is a U-shaped box with open ends and in its sides are slots opposite each other cut at 45-degree and 90-degree angles. These precisely cut slots guide a backsaw while cutting. The board or molding to be cut is placed against the back side or fence and clamped or held firmly in place. The saw is slipped into the proper slot and lowered onto the work. Clamp the miter box in a vise or to a workbench.

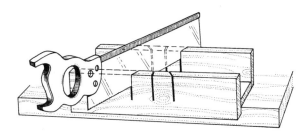

PLANES

Because planes were used for so many different tasks a large number of specialty planes evolved that have become popular collector items. A plane is a handheld tool that slides across wood to smooth and shape it. It has a front knob and back handle with a chisel-like blade in the center. This blade can be adjusted for depth depending on whether you want a smooth or rough cut. When not in use a plane should rest on its side; don't lay it down on its blade.

Two of the most basic planes used today are the bench and block planes. They can be used on repair and maintenance jobs around the house as well as for woodworking projects. Other planes are optional depending on your specific needs.

Bench Plane

A bench plane, also called a jack plane, is larger than a block plane and is used to smooth a long section of wood. It's useful to shorten a door that binds in its jamb or on the bottom, or to custom-fit landscape timbers.

To operate a bench plane, use both hands, one gripping the front knob and the other grasping the tote, or the back handle. Push or pull the plane over the surface, going with the grain of the wood. The wood being planed should be set firmly in a level position in a vise or clamp so it is secure as you work on it. Push the plane over the surface, removing curls of wood shavings as you work. Work from the outside to the middle and then turn the board around or reposition yourself so you can work from the opposite side toward the center. Do most of your planing with the wood grain to prevent the plane from tearing the wood.

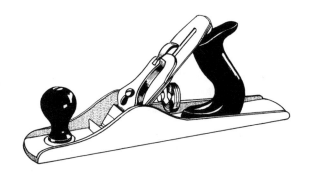

Block Plane

A block plane is a small plane that you operate with one hand. It is light and handy to use. Block planes are good for trimming the ends of

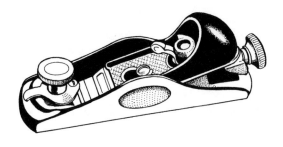

boards because the iron, or cutting blade, is placed at a lower angle to the wood than it would be on the larger bench planes.

This small plane comes in handy for doing odd jobs like repairing the frame of a wooden window screen or building a picture frame when wood joinery is involved. This type of plane can finesse a wooden shelf so it fits in a cabinet or help you patch a repair in a wooden floor.

When trimming the end of a board with a block plane work the plane from the outer edge toward the center of the board to prevent splitting the edge.

Rabbet Plane

This plane has a cutter that extends all the way to the side of the plane, which allows you to cut a rabbet, or groove, in the edge of a board. The rabbet plane has an adjustable fence, or bracket, that holds the plane square to the edge or end of the board and controls the width of the rabbet. It also has a depth gauge that regulates the depth of the rabbet the plane will cut. This plane can cut across the grain because it has a small spur cutter located in the body in front of the main cutter. The small spur scores the wood before the main cutter to prevent it

from tearing the wood as it moves across the grain.

The rabbet plane can also be used for other planing tasks that require a plane with a full-width cutter, such as trimming the shoulder of a tenon.

To use a rabbet plane set the fence to the width of the rabbet you want to make and then set the depth gauge to the depth of the cut. If you are cutting across the grain of the board, engage the spur cutter located on the side of the plane; otherwise it is not needed. You will find the plane works best if set up to remove a fine shaving. When using the plane put most of your pressure toward pushing the wood against the fence instead of pushing down on the plane.

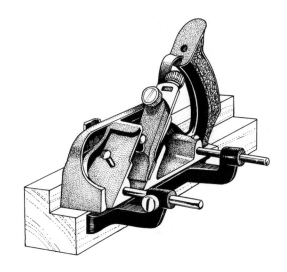

Clifton Multiplane

This is a specialty plane used by cabinetmakers and carpenters to create everything from intricate ceiling moldings to tongue-and-groove floorboards. This tool comes with a thorough explanation from its manufacturer about how to set up, operate, and adjust it.

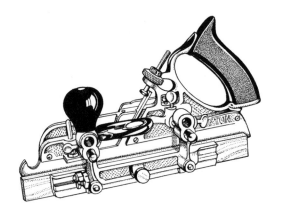

SAWS

Years ago handsaws were used for so many tasks they evolved into specialized tools. It wasn't unusual for a well-equipped carpenter to have a toolbox full of them. Today a handsaw is one of the most used tools when it comes to making a repair or building a project around your house.

The cutting tasks a saw can perform are determined by its teeth. Saws are rated by the number of teeth they have per inch of cutting edge. A saw with eight teeth per inch (or TPI) will not cut as smoothly as a saw with fourteen TPI. In general, the higher the TPI, the smoother the cut. But small teeth can't take a large bite out of the wood, so a smooth-cutting saw is also a slow-cutting saw.

If you look closely at the teeth you will notice that they are alternately bent slightly to opposite sides of the saw blade. This allows the path that the saw cuts through the wood,

called the kerf, to be slightly wider than the blade itself. This extra clearance helps keep the blade cutting freely as it moves through the wood.

It is not hard to see that a saw with a wide blade will naturally cut straight through wood because the blade is stiff and won't easily bend. Conversely, a saw with a narrow blade can cut curved paths through wood because the blade is narrow and provides little resistance to turning as it moves through the wood.

If used frequently, your saw blades should be sharpened by a professional sharpening service.

Before storing the tool, remove any sawdust on the blade and cover the saw with heavy cardboard or cloth. Keep the saw out of the rain, and if it does get rusty, wipe on a light oil such as WD-40.

The four saws described here will get you through most home repair and woodworking projects.

Crosscut Saw

Depending on the type of work you do around the house, the saw you use most will probably be the crosscut. This type of saw is used to cut a board to length and is the mainstay in jobs like cutting two-by-fours for framing a room or cutting stair treads to rebuild a back porch.

The teeth of a crosscut saw are sharpened to cut most efficiently across the wood grain; they look like sharp knife points. These pointed teeth cut the wood fibers as they tear into wood.

For general use around the house and workshop, purchase a crosscut saw with twelve teeth per inch. If you plan to do a lot of rough carpentry or deck framing get an additional saw with eight teeth per inch.

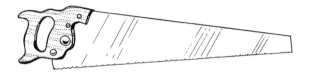

Ripsaw

Whenever you cut a board down its length you are cutting with the grain or making a rip cut. Since sawing down the length of a board can be a tedious task, the ripsaw is designed to cut wood along the grain as efficiently as possible.

A ripsaw looks like a crosscut saw, but it has teeth that are shaped to cut with the grain of the wood instead of across it. The teeth are larger and shaped more like chisels. This allows the teeth to gouge larger chunks of wood from the board, cutting it faster.

This saw is good for cutting sheets of plywood for an attic floor or for paneling, or whenever the job requires cutting across and parallel to the grain of the wood.

For all practical purposes a ripsaw with eight teeth per inch will serve you well.

Using a Crosscut Saw or Ripsaw

The most important factor in producing clean, smooth, accurate cuts with either of these saws is proper work support. Hold the wood close to the cut. If the piece is small and difficult to grasp, secure it with a clamp.

Use sawhorses. A good pair of sawhorses are useful for cutting large pieces of material such as plywood, paneling, or long pieces of framing lumber. They provide a sturdy platform for the material at a convenient work height. When working at a sawhorse, line yourself up so your body is perpendicular to the work. Don't lean over or work at an angle when using a saw, because it affects the angle of your cut in the wood.

See directions for building stackable sawhorses on page 138.

If the cutoff, or waste piece, is large, support it at the end to prevent it from pinching the saw blade as you cut through the board. The farther you cut into the board, the less wood is left to support the waste piece. If the board is more than a foot long, its weight causes it to sag, closing the slot, or kerf, that your saw is working in.

Cut wide of your layout lines. Mark the material accurately so you know where to cut and then place the saw blade on the waste side of this line. This is called "leaving the line," and it allows you to dress up or smooth the cut with a plane or sandpaper without making the board too short.

To start a cut begin sawing on the edge of the board to create a groove for the saw blade. Begin slowly with short strokes until the saw blade cuts smoothly with long strokes. Use guides made from straight scrap wood clamped along your layout line to help guide your saw. If your saw wanders astray slow down and back up slightly. Realign the blade and start again. Just before the cut is complete take hold of the waste end of the board so it doesn't fall and rip a splinter off the piece to be used.

Coping Saw

A coping saw has a very fine blade that is attached to a wide-open U-shaped frame on a handle. The thin blade is held tight by tension between the frame ends. The saw permits the cutting of intricate scrolls and delicate shapes and curves with control. It was originally designed for coping, or joining two molded strips of wood at an angle by fitting one over the other. A coping saw's frame, minus the handle, measures approximately 6⅜ inches long by 4¾ or 6¼ inches high. It's popular with woodworkers and craftspeople as well as those who are handy around the house.

Woodworkers use a coping saw to cut curved outlines, to fit moldings together, and to remove excess wood from intricate joinery. Craftspeople who build small objects such as dollhouse furniture and miniatures use a coping saw because it is lightweight and easy to manipulate in tight corners.

You operate the saw using both hands. Hold the handle in one hand and the top of the U-shaped frame with the other hand. As you work the saw apply only light pressure and concentrate on keeping the blade level and square. The saw can be turned and the blade swiveled to follow an intricate curve.

Because the blade is thin and delicate it can't be sharpened and must be replaced when dull. Replacing a blade requires a little coordination. Hold the handle against your stomach or leg and push the saw against a solid surface like a countertop. This action compresses the saw frame and relieves the tension on the blade so you can lift it out of the blade-retaining

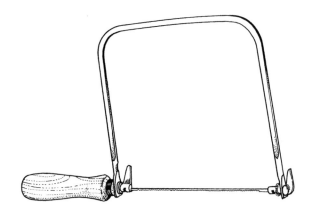

spigots. Insert the new blade into the spigots so the teeth are pointing toward the front of the saw. Replacement blades are available with 10, 15, and 20 teeth per inch. Again, the higher the number of teeth per inch, the finer the cut.

Backsaw

A backsaw is a very fine-toothed saw with a rectangular blade stiffened by a rigid metal strip along its back. It has a contoured hardwood handle for easy gripping and sawing. It is basically used for woodworking and finish carpentry and other fine joinery. Since it is frequently used with a miter box, a backsaw is sometimes referred to as a miter saw.

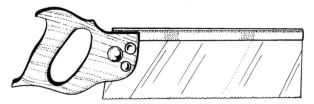

SCRAPERS

There are four types of scrapers that are very useful for the homeowner: hook scrapers, cabinet scrapers, shave hooks, and the common putty knife. You will invent your own uses for these handy tools, but primarily they are used to remove old paint, varnish, and glue without chemical solvents or any other unwanted buildup on wood. The first three types mentioned are specialty tools that can be found in any woodworker's store, home center, or hardware store. Putty knives can be found in any hardware store or home center. The secret to any scraping job is keeping the scraper sharp and choosing the right tool for the job at hand.

Hook Scrapers

A hook scraper, also called a paint scraper, has a handle that holds a removable metal blade. The blade is set at a right angle to the handle and is pulled along the surface you're scraping. The blade is approximately 2 inches wide and either slides into a slot in the handle or is held in place with a set screw. The handle is up to 10 inches long and can be made of metal, wood, or plastic.

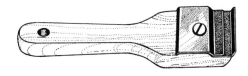

On old windows or doors, a hook scraper makes short work of getting rid of old paint, caulk, and dried-on foam weatherstripping.

When refinishing floors, the tool is useful for removing the finish in tight spots like underneath a radiator or around stair spindles.

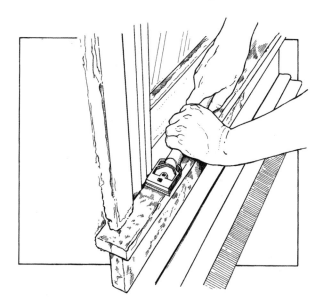

Use a hook scraper to remove a buildup of layers of paint on woodwork.

When using a long-handled scraper, put one hand at the neck of the scraper and the other at the end of the handle to apply pressure. Hold it almost perpendicular to the surface and try to work in long, smooth strokes, pulling the tool toward you and completing each stroke by lifting the tool upward. You'll feel the blade lift the finish from the surface. Handle a smaller scraper in the same way, using it to skim the surface of the finish and shave it off.

Throughout the job, keep the blade clean and free of any buildup. The blade will dull quickly, so touch it up often with a file. If it needs a more extensive sharpening, put the

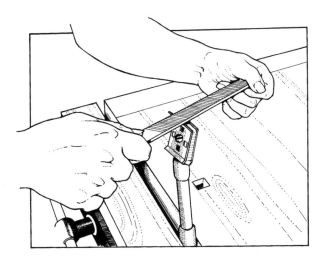

A sharp scraper works best, so stop often to sharpen the blade of your scraper with a file.

face. Cabinet scrapers remove a very fine layer of the wood's surface, which is often all that's needed to complete the job. They are sharpened with a burnishing technique. The edge of the scraper is filed flat and then a steel rod is drawn over one edge to create a razor-sharp lip.

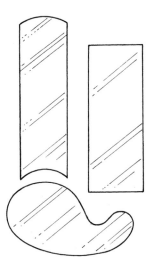

handle in a vise or clamp the tool to your workbench. When the blade has a uniform, shiny edge, remove it from the handle, turn it, and reinsert it in the opposite direction so you can sharpen the other side of the blade. The hook scraper is a rough cutting tool so it does not require a fine edge, just a sharp one.

Cabinet Scrapers

Cabinet scrapers are thin, flat plates of steel that come in various shapes. You'll see them sold individually and in packs of three, which usually include a rectangle or square and curved shapes. Woodworkers use these scrapers instead of sanding to create a flawless, smooth surface before applying a finish.

These scrapers are handy for giving a facelift to a butcher-block counter in the kitchen or for spot refinishing a tabletop or wood floor where you don't want to refinish the entire sur-

To use a cabinet scraper hold it firmly in both hands and push or pull it across the surface so it grazes the wood without gouging it. Hold it almost perpendicular to the surface and try to work in long, smooth strokes. Use your thumbs to apply greater pressure by positioning them low on the scraper. Always work the scraper with the grain of the wood. As you work across a surface complete each stroke by lifting the tool upward.

Shave Hooks

Shave hooks are for heavier work like removing paint or finish from a carved piece of wood, such

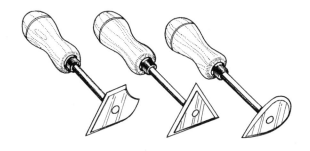

as molding or furniture, or for fine-finishing intricate wood where cabinet scrapers can't reach.

Shave hooks have wooden handles approximately 8 inches long and heavy shanks that hold odd-shaped metal scrapers. Their steel scraping blades are a combination of shapes—rounded, pointed, and straight—to smooth convex and concave surfaces. Depending on how you hold a shave hook, its cutting edge can be made to match just about any curved surface.

Choose a scraper with a curved blade to match a curved surface of molding or trim.

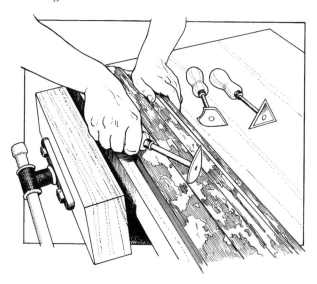

Hold the tool firmly by its handle and push or pull it at an angle while applying pressure. Be careful using the tool if you are uncertain as to whether you are working with a hard wood or a soft wood, as you can damage soft wood if you use the tool too roughly.

Putty Knives

A putty knife isn't really made to scrape surfaces but can be useful for easy jobs. This push-type scraper has a stiff, flat blade with a moderately sharp edge and will have a wood or plastic handle. It is effective in removing loose and flaking paint but can't lift old, hard paint very well. It can also be used for removing loose or already softened wallpaper.

SHARPENING STONE

Use a sharpening stone for chisels and the blades of knives, scrapers, and planes. There are three types, categorized by the lubricant that keeps metal from clogging the stone. An oilstone is coated with oil before sharpening, Japanese water stones are used with water (much neater than oil), and a ceramic stone is synthetic and is used alone. A typical sharpening stone is a block of wood with a two-sided stone, one side coarse for grinding and shaping a blade, the other finer for honing edges.

To sharpen a chisel place its bevel edge flat on the stone and then hone the blade by rubbing it across the stone, pulling it toward you or in a circular motion. Take care to maintain the same bevel angle. You can purchase a tool

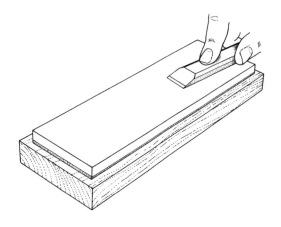

holder that will make this process easier. When all the nicks are removed and the edge of the chisel is straight and shiny, turn the chisel over, place the flat side of the chisel on the stone, and give it a couple of passes over the stone. This will remove the thin "wire" edge that was created when you honed the beveled side.

WOODWORKING VISE

A vise is a mechanical device for holding a piece of wood or metal while you work on it.

It has jaws that grip the object securely so you can work on it with both hands. It attaches to a workbench or table with a threaded main screw and a sliding steel handle. One jaw is permanent and the other moves back and forth depending on the size of the object being secured.

A woodworking vise has protective pieces of wood or plastic covering its jaws so they don't mar the wood. You can use a standard machinist vise for woodworking if you make a set of jaw protectors from scrap wood.

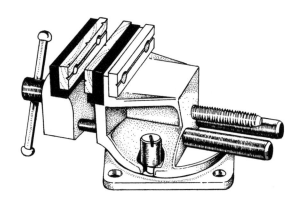

• PART TWO •

Home Repair and Improvement Projects

·Replicate Wooden Moldings·

Matching the molding in an old house can be a challenge, but it's often necessary to really make a room complete. This project comes up in a variety of ways. Remodeling often means tying a new addition to an existing house, which is nicely accomplished with moldings that flow continuously between the new and old parts of the house. If you remove a cabinet that had been built into a wall you may be faced with a section of wall without floor and ceiling moldings. Installing duplicate moldings to match what's there is the solution. And when a section of molding is damaged by water from a leaky roof, replacing it is the answer.

If you are duplicating molding to trim out an entire door or window in a room, you don't have to be fussy if the contour of the molding isn't exactly like the original because it will not be placed close to the original. However, if you're patching in a piece of molding to fill a missing section you must be more precise.

Even though lumberyards carry a wide selection of molding profiles it's often difficult to find an exact duplication of molding installed fifty or more years ago. You can sidestep the problem by removing all the old woodwork and replacing it with new, but that's expensive and a tremendous waste of wonderful old wood trim. A better choice is to keep the original woodwork and make a short section to match it.

In the old days most moldings were custom-made on-site by carpenters with hand planes. Today you can duplicate short sections of moldings with a hand plane similar to the original tool. Molding planes are expensive, but you can find them used if you shop flea markets and house sales. The plane we used is a Clifton Multiplane, which is a copy of a hundred-year-old design.

Another approach to duplicating molding patterns is to combine readily available moldings into custom configurations. The best application of this technique is when you're installing all-new trim in a room and making large quantities of molding with a hand plane is not practical.

Duplicating an Old Piece of Molding

A hand plane and cabinet scrapers are the tools of choice to duplicate old molding. Your workbench becomes engulfed with the aroma of the wood shavings as you work the tools through the wood, custom-shaping it to match the original.

The traditional method of making molding is to use specially shaped wooden planes. At the turn of the century the well-tooled craftsman began to replace his wide selection of molding planes with a single multipurpose plane that is reproduced today as the Clifton Multiplane. Fitted with its various blades (plow, beading, and fluting cutters), the Multiplane can duplicate a wide variety of moldings.

To duplicate a piece of molding you need a short section of the original to use as a pattern. If the existing molding is varnished or coated with some other clear finish and you can see the wood grain, choose a matching type of wood. If the new molding will be painted, make it from a piece of poplar, which machines nicely and produces a smoother and cleaner cut than pine.

TRANSFER THE PROFILE

In order to duplicate the existing molding you must first transfer its contour to a piece of heavy paper or lightweight cardboard. Hold the paper tight against the end of the old molding and trace the molding's shape onto the paper with a marker or pencil. Then cut the image of the molding from the paper.

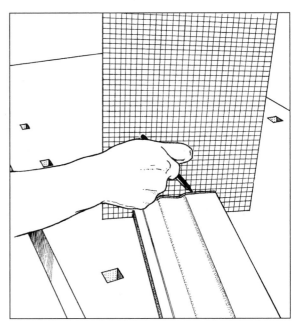

Hold a piece of cardboard against the end of the existing molding and trace its profile on the cardboard.

Use the positive pattern (the piece that has the curves bulging out) to decide which plane cutters best fit the molding contour and to position the plane. Use the negative part of the pattern to check the molding's contour as you work.

To help you select the best plane cutters to

use, place each plane on the pattern. Move them around so their profiles match the curve of the molding. Use your imagination during this process because none of the cutters will be a perfect fit. The flat-cutting plow cutters are used to remove excess stock and to create beading. Fluting cutters hollow out concave grooves, ovolo cutters cut contours, and beading cutters cut convex curves. By combining these basic shapes you can duplicate a wide variety of moldings. Remember, you probably will not find a perfect match; look for the closest match. You can use a cabinet scraper to do the final shaping.

When you've found the combination of plane cutters needed, mark the center line of each cutter with a marker. Then position the cutter on the pattern and transfer the position of the center line you drew on the cutter to the pattern.

Next, transfer the position of the cutter center lines from the pattern to the end of the board. Use these lines as a guide when you are adjusting the fence of the Multiplane. Place the plane over the mark and move the fence into position so the center mark on the plane's cutter is in alignment with the mark on the end of the board. As you work your way across the

Place the Multiplane cutters against the molding profile to find the best fit, then mark the center of each cutter on the pattern.

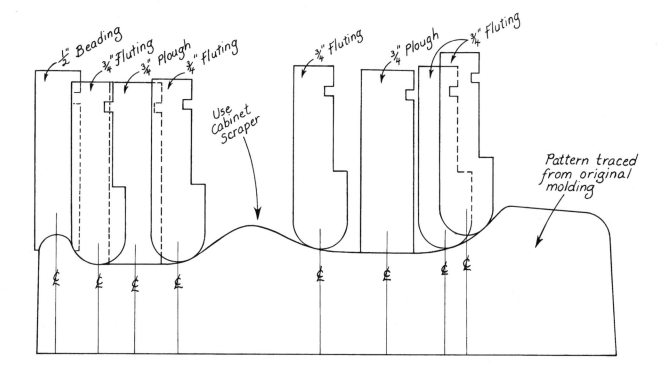

board you can change cutters as needed and align them with the proper mark on the end of the board before you start the new cut.

The Multiplane cuts quickly with sharp cutters. When reproducing a wide molding like the one shown, use the ¾-inch-wide plow cutter to pare down the flat areas rather than the wider plow cutters. This cutter is easier to push than the wider cutters, so take the easy way since you have a lot of planing to do.

Start each new cut with the Multiplane about a foot back from the front end of the board. After a couple of passes move the plane back to make the cut longer, gradually extend-ing your plane strokes farther and farther up the board. This allows the plane to gradually cut deeper and deeper as you work your way up the board. You don't have to worry about cutting too deeply because the plane will stop cutting when the foot of the depth gauge comes in contact with the wood. After the molding is roughed out with the plane, do the final shaping with a cabinet scraper.

FINISHING

An inexpensive set of three cabinet scrapers allows you to quickly remove rough and uneven marks left by the plane. The scrapers remove stock faster than sandpaper and can be used for final shaping of the molding. A set of three cabinet scrapers is available at most large home centers or hardware stores.

The flat and curved cabinet scrapers are handy for smoothing rounded areas and for removing the cutting marks left by the plane. The most useful scraper is shaped like a French curve with edges that have a changing radius. Depending on how you hold it, a wide variety of contours can be smoothed. Hold the tool at about a 30-degree angle to the wood and drag it across the surface. The sharp edge will cut a small curl of wood similar to a plane shaving. Smoothing and shaping the molding with one of these tools is much faster than with sandpaper.

After final scraping, give the molding a light sanding. Use a contour sanding pad or wrap

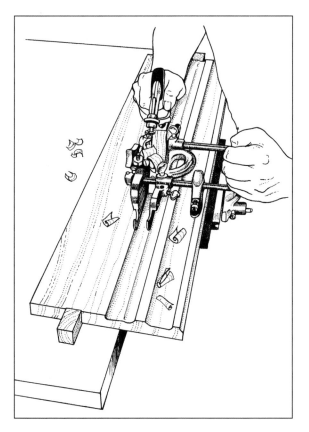

Start planing with short strokes and gradually work back farther up the board to keep the plane cutting.

sandpaper around a sponge to sand in the convex areas. A light sanding is all that is necessary.

Install the straight pieces of new molding after carefully measuring and cutting them to length. If the molding is large, use 8d finish nails, otherwise use 6d finish nails. Use your nail set to drive the heads of the nails below the surface of the molding and then fill the holes with wood putty. Seal any gaps between the wall and the wood with caulk.

If you're using the molding as a patch-in section between two pieces of old molding, measure it accurately before cutting. Use sandpaper to remove any glue or dirt from the ends of the old molding so the surfaces are clean wood. Sand the ends of the new molding and fit it in carefully.

Creating Custom Moldings with Standard Pieces

You can create your own crown moldings by piecing together different styles of moldings. Molding is stocked at lumberyards and home centers stacked in bins and sold in lengths varying from 3 to 16 feet.

To estimate how many feet of molding you need, measure the room and add up the length of each wall. Molding is priced by the foot, so if you know the number of feet you need, you can multiply it by the cost per foot to get an estimate of the cost of the material.

When looking at pieces of molding notice the difference between "clear," flawless material

and the less expensive but rougher finger-jointed material. If the molding will be painted and not finished naturally you can save considerably by buying the lesser-grade material since you'll never see the surface of the wood after it is painted.

Most lumberyards have an overall general reference chart called "Molding Profiles," which shows a profile of each molding with a stock number to identify it. Some yards have a display featuring all the moldings they carry and those they can special-order for you. These displays are usually made from short sections of moldings to illustrate their profiles. This is very helpful when creating a custom molding because you can trace contours on a piece of paper and then combine different shapes to form a new profile.

You can combine moldings with other dimensional lumber such as one-by-threes and one-by-fours to make very ornate ceiling cornice moldings. To visualize what one of these custom moldings will look like, take short sections of molding and lay them down on a flat surface.

To learn how to trim out a room with ceiling moldings, refer to page 36, which explains the techniques of cutting, fitting, and installing molding in place.

Here are two combinations of standard molding to make a custom baseboard molding for the floor and an elaborate crown ceiling molding. This technique is used most often for trimming out an entire room in an old house when you want the molding to be in keeping with what's in other rooms in the house.

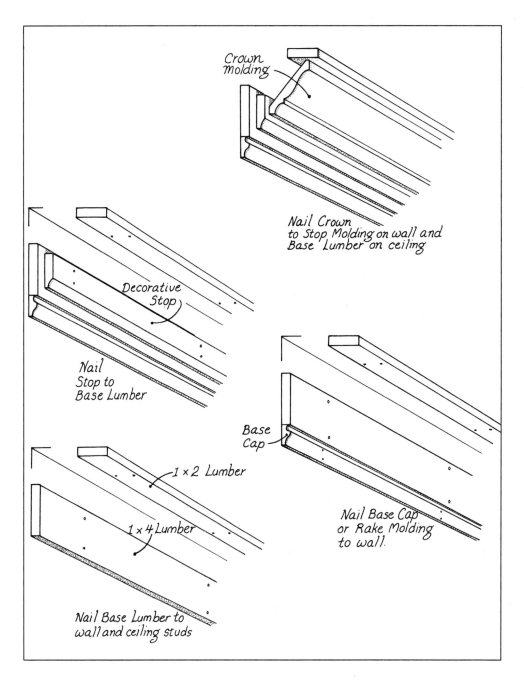

Crown Molding

Nail Crown
to Stop Molding on wall and
Base Lumber on ceiling

Decorative Stop

Nail
Stop to
Base Lumber

Base Cap

1 x 2 Lumber

1 x 4 Lumber

Nail Base Cap
or Rake Molding
to wall.

Nail Base Lumber to
wall and ceiling studs

Wide, fancy crown molding can be made by combining stock molding with dimensional lumber. Use common one-by-four and one-by-two stock for the base.

Baseboard Molding

Combine one-by-six lumber, which is actually 5½ inches high, with standard base cap molding for an attractive baseboard trim that looks like the original moldings found in many older houses. The lumber is ¾ inch thick topped with base cap molding that is slightly narrower, so it creates a pleasing recessed detail. When painted the combined trim looks like one piece.

If you have an older house with uneven floors, consider installing base shoe molding. This is a small flexible molding installed at the foot of the large base. Unlike the stiff one-by-six base molding, it can be bent to follow the contour of the floor and conceal any gaps between the base and floor. Don't use a base shoe if you plan to install carpeting in the room.

Crown Molding

To duplicate fancy crown molding use stock one-by-two and one-by-four lumber as a base with a combination of stop, base cap, and crown moldings. This buildup creates a very intricate ceiling molding. First, install the one-by-two lumber on the ceiling and the one-by-four boards on the walls. Then nail the base cap molding to the wall under the one-by-four base and the stop molding to the face of one-by-fours on the wall. Finally, nail the crown molding to the one-by-twos on the ceiling and the face of the stop.

These are only two combinations, which should give you an idea of what is possible. To help you install the moldings with the proper spacing cut a short piece of each molding and arrange the pieces on a sheet of paper as you want them to be on the ceiling and wall. Then trace their profiles on the paper. Use this pattern to position the one-by-two and one-by-four nailers on the wall and ceiling and to position the other moldings as you build up the different layers.

·Install Wainscoting in a Room·

Wainscoting was used as a rich, warm wall treatment covering the lower third of walls in the library or study of older houses. This wood paneling was traditionally custom-made at the job site by craftspeople. Using hand planes, carpenters cut beading in the surface of the board and tongue-and-groove edges along each board and joined them together. They cut, fit, and planed the boards and then nailed them to the wall framing.

Today you have more choices when it comes to installing wainscoting in a room. If you have the skills and time you can custom-build wainscoting like the craftsmen of old, but if you're not an experienced carpenter you might be interested in two other options.

You can buy 4-by-8-foot plywood panels etched with vertical grooves to simulate the look of tongue-and-groove boards and hang half sheets of the paneling topped by a chair rail. Another alternative, one we prefer because you work with individual boards, is using beaded plank paneling kits. These kits contain 8-foot lengths of beaded pine milled with edge and center beads that can be easily cut using a handsaw. They are sold at home centers and lumberyards and are available in various sizes and wood species. The 3³⁄₁₆-inch-wide planks are easy to work with and install.

The thin planks can be glued to almost any sound surface with construction adhesive after removing the base molding that runs along the floor. You can then reinstall that molding over the wainscoting and finish off the top edge with a panel cap or chair rail molding.

This thinner version of wainscoting boards can be installed directly on most wall surfaces without conflicting with window and door trim. This simplifies the job considerably. To install heavier (¾-inch or thicker) boards as wainscoting, the wallboard behind it should be removed so the boards can be hung directly on the studs, flush with the door and window trim.

Wainscoting is usually about 3 feet high because its function is to protect the wall from the bumps and nicks of furniture such as the back of a chair pushing away from a dining table. Since most of these planks come in 8-foot lengths you can get at least two pieces out of each one.

Prepare the Wall

In almost every situation you will find that it is easier to remove the baseboard molding and reinstall it over new wainscoting than to put the wainscoting on top of the baseboard. The results are also better-looking. If you work slowly you'll find that it's not difficult to remove the baseboard without damaging it. The best tools to use are a small pry bar and a putty knife. You do the least amount of damage to the molding if you pull it off the wall with the nails intact (and remove them later) or pull the molding off the wall leaving the nails in the wall. This works only if the nails used are finish nails without heads.

Place the putty knife between the pry bar and the wall to protect its surface and the baseboard. Start at one end and work slowly, easing the baseboard away from the wall. Don't try to pry it off the wall by pulling on one end because you will break the molding. You can apply pressure with short pulls to loosen it from the wall, but use the pry bar on any tight nails.

When the baseboard is free from the wall, remove any nails remaining in the wall with a hammer. Protect the wall surface with a rag or piece of heavy cardboard as you use the claw end of the hammer to remove the nails. Do the same thing with nails in the baseboard. Hammer them from the backside of the baseboard, forcing them out on their finished side. Set the molding aside for reinstallation later.

Remove any wallpaper or loose and flaking paint from the wall where the wainscoting is planned. When the wall is smooth and structurally sound begin to plan the layout.

Layout

To help you align the boards accurately, make a level line across the wall at the height of the top edge of the wainscoting. The easiest way to do this is with a chalk line. For example, if you want wainscoting to be 32 inches high (a traditional height), go to each corner of the wall and measure 32 inches up from the floor and mark the wall. Then stretch the chalk line between the marks and snap it to transfer the chalk to the wall. Use this line for aligning the boards.

Measure the width of a wall and divide it by the width of the plank to give you a rough idea of how the spacing will work out. Another method is to line up the planks against the wall just as they will be installed. Ideally you should have planks of equal width at each end of a wall, but it will not be noticeable if they are not exactly the same. You may find it is better to cut down the first plank you install if there is a very thin piece needed to fill a small gap at the other end of the wall. It is easier to cut 1½ inches off a board than to try to cut a ¾-inch strip to squeeze into a small gap.

Prefinish Wainscoting

Unfinished pine planks can be painted or stained or left natural, depending on your choice of finish. If you choose to paint, use a primer coat first; for staining use a wood conditioner to avoid blotches on the wood.

Prefinish the panels or planks before installation so you can lay them on a flat surface, where it is easier to apply paint or stain. You can also apply finish to the tongue edge of the board so if it shrinks during the dry winter months the slight gap that opens between the boards will not expose unfinished wood.

Another idea is to prefinish the planks with their primer coat and then apply the topcoat after the wainscoting is installed.

Install the Wainscoting

Cut the planks to length with a ten-point or finer crosscut handsaw. Using a miter box will give you nice square ends on the cuts. But since the top and bottom of the planks will be covered by molding you don't have to be too particular with this cut.

Before you install a plank note that each

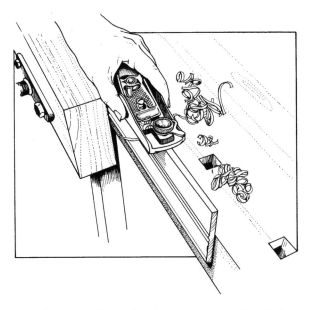

Trim the tongue off one edge of the wainscoting with a block or bench plane so it will fit flush against the wall or woodwork.

edge of the wainscoting has a bevel on it. Use your block or bench plane to plane the groove side of the first board flat so it will fit flush against door trim or tight into a corner.

Measure and cut the planks to length for a 2- to 3-foot section of wall at a time. Test-fit the planks on the wall to make sure that they fit and then install them with construction adhesive.

The planks are glued to the wall with construction adhesive, which comes in tubes. Since the wood is not heavy, a ¼-inch bead of adhesive will hold it in place. Cut the tip off the nozzle at a 45-degree angle to make a ¼-inch opening in the tip. Then break the tube seal by pushing a piece of wire through the hole in the tip nozzle.

Apply the adhesive to the back of the board around its perimeter and then go back across the board in a zigzag pattern. Then put the

Trim Out the Wall

After the wainscoting is glued to the walls it's time to install the top molding. Lumberyards stock a molding called panel cap that is designed to go on top of paneling and fit nicely over wainscoting. Install this molding with the same construction adhesive, using a few 6d finish nails to hold it in place while the adhesive sets up. See the section on trimming out a room for tips on making coped corner joints.

Install panel cap molding on the top of wainscoting with 6d finish nails. Sink the nail head with a nail set.

Use a caulk gun to apply a bead of construction adhesive to the back of the wainscoting.

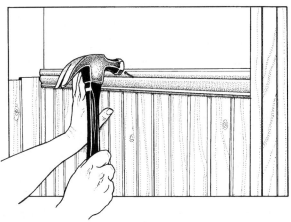

board in position and press it into place. Make sure you align it with the chalk line and that it is butting tightly against the trim or adjoining wall.

•Trim Out a Room with•
Ceiling Molding

Ceiling molding does a lot for a room. Look at identical rooms, one with molding and the other without, and see how different they appear. Without any defining features the walls and ceilings of a room blend together. Even when walls are painted a different color from the ceiling, the room has no definitive edges.

A room with molding, however, is well defined. When painted the same color as the wall, molding defines the space by creating neat and precise borders. When painted in a contrasting color, molding is bolder and outlines a room, calling attention to whatever architectural features it possesses.

Many older homes have rooms already appointed with molding, some ornate and intricate. While a new custom-built home will often have molding, you won't find it in most new homes. But it can easily be added to give a room a custom touch. All it takes is a few hand tools, a stepladder, and the help of someone to hold long pieces of molding during installation.

Measuring a Room for Ceiling Molding

To buy ceiling molding for a room, measure the length of each wall, rounding it up to a whole number, and add 2 feet. Then add the four wall lengths together to know how much is needed. The extra molding will allow for some miscuts when you are making the mitered and coped joints.

Using a Miter Box

Making accurate square and angled cuts is the key to successful trim work. Toward this end you will find the miter box is probably your most useful tool. The miter box does not have to be fancy to be accurate, but if you are planning to do a lot of trim work—like installing baseboards, door and window trim, and other moldings—then the investment in a good quality miter box will be repaid many times over.

Accurate adjustable miter boxes have been around for a long time and can be purchased at most hardware stores or home centers. They usually come with a backsaw designed to fit the miter box. The saw is also movable, so it can be set at any angle. These tools are very versatile, especially if you are installing moldings or trim in an older house that does not have perfectly square walls.

On the other hand, a simple, inexpensive wooden miter box will make accurate cuts, and for the most part we recommend that you start off with one of these for most of the projects in this book. We suggest that you purchase a bench and block plane with the savings and make the shooting boards described in this book on pages 134–37. Even the best miter boxes can't produce as fine a miter as you can make if you dress up your cut with your plane and miter shooting board after it comes out of the wooden miter box.

The secret to using any miter box is to place the molding, or whatever you are going to cut, into the box correctly to hold it securely in place. At times the placement of a piece of molding in a miter box can get confusing, espe-cially when it is crown molding, which does not lie flat against the wall but is installed against the wall and ceiling. The trick to remember is to place molding in a miter box exactly as it will be when it is installed on the wall. With ceiling molding consider the bot-tom, or bed, of the miter box as the wall and the fence as the ceiling. Cutting at a 45-degree angle will give you a compound miter cut. For baseboard or floor moldings consider the base as the floor and the fence as the wall.

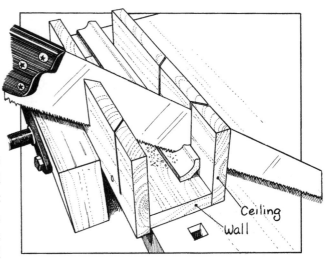

Put the molding in a miter box as if you were installing it on the wall. Think of the bottom of the box as the wall and the fence as the ceiling.

Cutting Square

Square, accurate cuts are easy to make using a miter box because it keeps the saw perpendicu-lar to the work while holding the saw blade straight as it cuts through the wood. To cut dimensional lumber and square molding stock, place the wood in the miter box with its wide side on the base, flush against the fence. If it's a large piece of wood, clamp it to the miter box base to hold it firmly in place. This way you can concentrate on cutting and not have to worry about holding the piece in place.

Wide crown and other moldings should also be clamped in place. You can clamp a piece of scrap to the miter box base so it holds the base of the molding in place. Then apply firm pressure with your hand to hold its upper edge against the fence.

The backsaw used with a miter box has fine teeth and is easy to start cutting with. Start your cut by pulling the saw backward (toward you) for a few strokes before you begin cutting. When you have created a small groove, lightly push the saw down and forward to cut.

Cutting Angles

Once you are set up to make square cuts with the miter box, cutting an angle is a simple matter of changing the angle of the saw if you are using an adjustable model. If you are using a wood miter box, place the saw in the proper angled slot.

It is very important that you hold the wood firmly in place when cutting an angle. The saw is moving through the wood at an angle so there is considerably more friction between the saw and wood than when making a square cut. If the wood shifts during the cut the angle will be off.

This is especially true when cutting angles in crown moldings since the saw is slicing through two different planes. With any movement of the molding, the miter box, or the fence and base, the cut will be off and the joint will be open.

Splicing Moldings

Ideally, when installing molding, you should use a single piece, but on a long wall that may be impossible. One of the popular techniques for installing moldings is using the miter box to splice two pieces of molding together.

The splice joint is nothing more than two opposite 45-degree cuts in the ends of the molding to be joined. One molding overlaps the other, hiding any gap that may open up as the wood dries out during the winter heating season. If the moldings were simply butting each other, this shrinking would open up a visible gap between them.

To make a splice joint, place the molding in the miter box with the back of the molding tight against the fence. Cut through the molding at a 45-degree angle. Then place the end of the other molding into the miter box in the same way and make the cut from the other end of the miter box, creating a mating 45-degree angle in its end.

Install the section of molding with the 45-degree cut that shows the molding's profile. This piece will have the point of the angle lying against the wall. Then install the other piece over the first. The overlapping of the joint will help hide any gap opened when the boards shrink.

Mitering a Corner

If the ends of two pieces of wood are cut with equal angles (usually 45 degrees, to form a square corner) and joined together, they form a miter joint. This joint is not hard to make with a miter box, but sometimes it can get a little confusing as to which way to cut the angles.

When mitering floor or wall moldings, always think of the back fence of the miter box as the wall. For example, to miter two pieces of base molding to form a 90-degree corner, you should place the back of the molding that forms the left half of the joint against the left fence of your miter box. Then move the saw guide to position the backsaw so that its handle swings away from the molding and the cut angles in toward the fence. If you are using a simple wooden miter box, use the set of guide slots at the right side of the miter box. Do the opposite to cut the other angle: position the right molding against the right fence and move the backsaw to the left.

Hold—or, better yet, clamp—the molding firmly against the fence as you cut. Don't force the saw through the cut. Allow the miter box to guide it for a more accurate cut.

Coping a Corner

Large moldings like 6-inch-high baseboards or crown molding are usually joined with miter joints at outside corners, but professional carpenters use a coping joint for inside corners.

This joint will not show any gap that may open up as the molding shrinks or expands with seasonal temperature changes.

Making a coped joint is a two-step process. First, cut a 45-degree angle on the end of a piece of molding that exposes its contour, then use a coping saw to cut along this contour to form the joint.

Place the molding in your miter box with its back against the fence just as it will be positioned on the wall. Then cut a 45-degree angle on the end of the molding. The saw handle should be moved away from the end of the molding so the cut will produce an angle with its point against the fence.

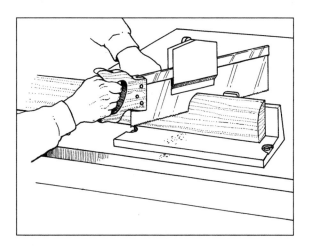

When coping a corner, adjust the miter box saw handle away from the end of the molding so the point of the miter is against the fence.

Then place the molding back down on a flat surface and cut along the edge of the 45-degree cut that outlines the molding contour. Angle the saw back toward the molding to undercut

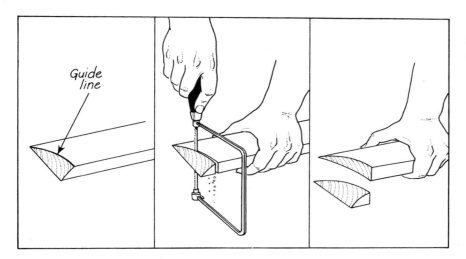

With a coping saw, undercut the joint slightly by angling the saw back toward the molding.

the joint slightly. When you have finished the cut, dress the joint with a piece of sandpaper until it matches the molding contour.

The joint is formed on the wall by cutting the end of one piece of molding square and installing it with its end flush into the corner. Then the piece of molding with the coped end is fitted over the other piece, concealing the joint. With a coped joint the shrinkage of only one piece of molding will tend to open the joint.

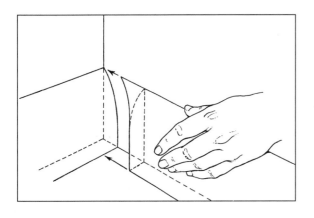

To install baseboard molding on an inside corner, fit the piece with the coped end over the square cut piece to conceal it.

Nailing Moldings

Moldings are usually held in place with finish nails. Use 6d finish nails for baseboards and window casing. On smaller moldings like base shoe use 4d finish nails, and on thin moldings like narrow cove and screen bead use wire brads.

Most of the molding available today is made of pine. This softwood can easily be marred by a misplaced hammer blow. To prevent this don't try to drive the finish nail all the way into the molding with your hammer. Instead, leave the nail head protruding slightly and drive the finish nail slightly below the surface of the wood with a nail set.

Finishing Moldings

You can finish molding with paint, either matching the walls and ceiling or creating a contrast with dramatic colors. Use stain to give moldings a rich, natural wood look. When using pine molding and finishing with stain, use a wood conditioner first because it prevents blotches, especially around knots and other imperfections in the wood.

·Build a Screen Door·

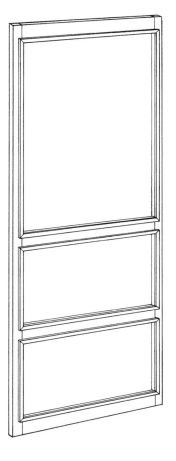

This simple wooden door is an alternative to a run-of-the-mill aluminum or vinyl screen door. Wooden screen doors are available in lumberyards in a few stock sizes, but we found the selection of sizes to be very limited. If you live in an older house with doorway openings that have settled or sag, you can use this design and alter the dimensions to fit the opening.

The door is made from screen stock, which is carried by most lumberyards and home centers. If they do not have this type of lumber you can substitute dimensional lumber, which is slightly thicker. Use two-by-three lumber for the stiles and two-by-four lumber for the rails. The stiles are 1½ inches thick compared with 1 1⁄16 inches for the screen stock, but the length of the door parts will not have to be altered. Check to make sure the wood you purchase is straight, not twisted. If there are knots make sure that they are small and tight.

This door is sized to fit an older house with an opening smaller than those found in most newer homes. Most doors are 80 inches high but vary in width from 30 to 36 inches. If your door is wider than 30 inches, increase the length of the rails from 26½ to 28½ inches for a 32-inch door and to 32½ inches for a 36-inch door.

If your door opening is an odd size and will not allow you to use any of these standard sizes, then build the door to the standard size larger than your opening and cut it down slightly to fit. It is better to have the door slightly larger than the jamb it fits into so it can be trimmed or planed to exact size.

The stiles are joined to the rails with a simple doweled joint formed with ½-inch diameter, 3-inch-long dowels. Most lumberyards stock a selection of precut dowels, but if yours doesn't, purchase several 3-foot-long hardwood dowels and cut your own.

How to Build It

Cut the stiles to the length specified in the parts list on page 47 first. Then lay out the rails and cut them to length. It is important that the ends of the rails are square to form a tight joint against the stiles. The best way to get a nice square end is to cut slightly outside the layout line and then place the board on your bench and square up its end with your plane. See pages 133–37 for how to make a bench hook and shooting board for this purpose.

Lay out the dowel locations on the stiles first and then transfer their locations to the ends of the rails. There are four rails—at the top, in the center at the doorknob area or lock, a kick rail near the bottom, and another at the bottom.

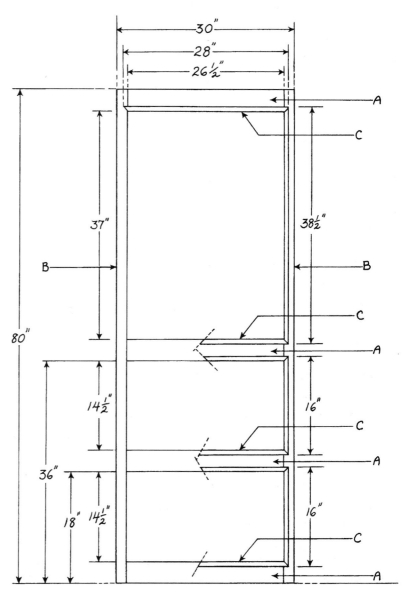

Clamp the two stiles together with their ends flush. Then mark the location of the top and bottom rails on each end. Measure 18 inches up from the bottom of the stile and mark the location of the bottom edge of the kick rail. Use a try square to make a straight line across both stiles. The rails are 3½ inches wide, so make another line 3½ inches above this line to define the location of the kick rail. Lay out the location of the lock rail in the same way. Its bottom edge is 36 inches up from the bottom of the door.

After you have marked the locations of all four rails on the edges and sides of both stiles, lay out the position of the dowels. There are three dowels per joint placed on ⅞-inch centers. Mark the location of the center dowel on the edges of the stiles. Then measure from this point ⅞ inch in either direction to mark the location of the others. Do the same at each of the rail locations on the stiles. The dowel spacing does not have to be exact, but the location of each dowel must be the same on each stile or the rails will not be straight. Also mark the dowel locations on the sides of the stiles.

Next transfer the location of the dowels from the stiles to the rails. The easiest way to do this is to place the stiles on a flat surface and position the rails between them. Then check that everything is square and transfer the dowel locations from the sides of the stiles to the sides of the rails. Then bring the layout lines on the sides of the rails around to their ends. This all sounds a little complicated, but it is not difficult if you work slowly and use a try square to draw straight layout lines from one piece to another.

Drilling the holes for the dowels is relatively easy, but you have to make sure the holes are drilled straight. If you are very careful you can drill these holes freehand, but a doweling jig will assure proper alignment. Follow the manufacturer's directions for using the jig since there are many different types available. The easiest to use is the self-centering type that clamps itself to the board. All you have to do is align the jig with your layout lines, place the drill into the guide, and drill the hole. In this case drill the holes slightly deeper than the dowels by at least 1½ inches.

Assembly should be done on a large, flat surface. Place all the parts in position and check the dowel alignment between the stiles and rails. Then apply glue to the edge of a stile in the area where the top rail makes contact. Place a small amount of glue in the dowel holes and spread it around with a scrap of wood. Then

Assemble the door by tapping the dowels in the rails into mating holes of the stiles. Protect the stile from the mallet blows with a scrap of wood.

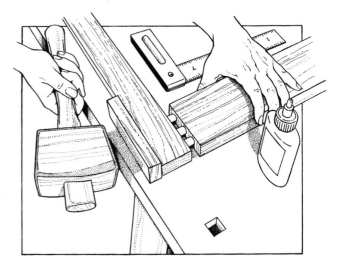

tap the dowels into the holes. Do the same to the other joint areas on the stile.

Apply glue to the ends of the rails and the dowel holes. Then place the rail in position and push it down over the dowels. You may have to pound on the other end of the rail to drive it home, but be sure to protect that end of the rail from damage with scrap wood or heavy cardboard. Proceed to install the other rails in the same way and then repeat this process on the other side.

While the glue dries, clamp the joints tightly. The best tool for this job is a pipe clamp. Place a pipe clamp at each joint between the stiles and rails. Protect the edges of the stiles from being dented by the clamps by placing small pieces of wood between them and the clamp face. To maintain even clamping pressure alternate the locations of the pipes. Put the first clamp in place; then position the second clamp so its pipe is on the other side of the door, alternating the position of the pipes as you secure each one. After the glue has dried use a sharp chisel to chip away any excess glue that might have squeezed out of the joints.

Cut the screen bead to length, miter the corners, and test the fit of each piece. They should frame the openings with the inside edge flush with the edges of the rails and stiles. But don't install the bead yet. First paint or stain the door frame and the screen bead before adding the screening.

When the paint or stain has dried apply screening fabric to the face of the door. It is held in place by the screen bead, which is tacked over it (this makes it easy to repair). We found the easiest and best method for installing

The rough edges of the screening are concealed with horizontal and vertical screen beads nailed in place.

the fabric is to tack it in place as a single piece and then trim away the excess after the screen bead is secured.

To install the screening, place the door frame on a flat surface and unroll the fabric onto the door frame. Align it carefully so it is straight and taut. Then nail on the top horizontal screen bead with 1-inch wire brads spaced about 1 inch apart. To stretch the screening fabric across the door, wrap one end of it around a piece of scrap wood so you can get a good grip and exert an even pull. Have a helper pull the end of the fabric tight while you install the bottom piece of screen bead. When the screen is tight and straight and secure at the top and bottom, install the other horizontal beads. Then install the vertical screen beads in opposing pairs and trim the screening flush with the outer edges of the beading with a sharp utility knife.

Hanging the Door

Next on the agenda: install the door in its opening. The hinges will be placed 5 inches from the top of the door and 10 inches from the bottom. First make sure that the door fits the jamb and then lay out the hinge locations on both the jamb and door at the same time. To do this, place the door in the jamb and put a couple of shims (thin pieces of wood to raise it up as if it were on its hinges) under it to allow for clearance at the bottom and sides. Use a hinge as a guide by placing it 5 inches down from the top of the door. Then mark the location of the top and bottom of the hinge on the

Use a combination square to lay out the hinge mortise. Set the blade to the width of the hinge and then transfer this measurement to the edge of the door and door jamb.

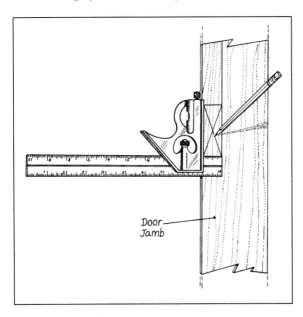

Door
Jamb

door and jamb at the same time. Repeat the same at the bottom, placing the hinge 10 inches from the bottom of the door.

Next lay out the hinge mortise location on the edge of the door. The mortise is a cut-out area in the wood where the hinge is installed. Remember, the barrel of the hinge should point to the outside face of the door. Use a combination square to transfer the line from the face of the door to its edge. Then set the blade of the combination square so that it protrudes out of the square 1 inch. Use the blade to guide your knife as you scribe a line 1 inch in from the face of the door. Put the hinge in place so its top edge is aligned with the layout line transferred from the door face and scribe along the side of the hinge to outline it.

Adjust the blade of your combination square so it protrudes ⅛ inch from the square and use it as a guide to lay out the depth of the mortise. Then make a series of shallow parallel cuts with your 1-inch chisel along the hinge layout. With your chisel remove the wood chips by cutting in from the edge of the door at the layout line scribed on the face of the door. Then smooth the bottom of the mortise with the chisel blade. Cut the hinge mortise at the other end of the door in the same way and then make the mortise in the jamb.

Pull the pins out of the hinges to separate them into two halves and install one side on the door and the other on the jamb. Then hang the door in the jamb. Most screen doors are held shut with a door spring or closer; either one will work fine here. Latch the door shut with a traditional hook and eye or purchase a latching handle at your local lumberyard or home center.

TOOLS

Hammer

Saw

Brace and bits

Doweling jig

Chisel

Combination square

Pipe clamp

Utility knife

Mallet

PARTS LIST

	Part	Number	Size	Material
A	rail	4	$1\frac{1}{16}'' \times 3\frac{1}{2}'' \times 26\frac{1}{2}''$	pine
B	stile	2	$1\frac{1}{16}'' \times 1\frac{3}{4}'' \times 80''$	pine
C	horizontal bead	6	$\frac{1}{2}'' \times \frac{3}{4}'' \times 28''$	pine
D	upper vertical bead	2	$\frac{1}{2}'' \times \frac{3}{4}'' \times 38\frac{1}{2}''$	pine
E	lower vertical bead	4	$\frac{1}{2}'' \times \frac{3}{4}'' \times 16''$	pine

MATERIALS LIST

Material	Amount	Size	Used For
screen stock	14 feet	$1\frac{1}{16}'' \times 1\frac{3}{4}''$	stiles
screen stock	12 feet	$1\frac{1}{16}'' \times 3\frac{1}{2}''$	rails
screen bead	32 feet	$\frac{1}{4}'' \times \frac{3}{4}''$	screen
hinges and screws	2	$3''$	
carpenter's glue	1 bottle		
wood dowels	24	$\frac{1}{2}''$	
wire brads	1 box	$\frac{3}{4}''$	
fiberglass screen	1	8-foot roll	

· Renew a Window ·

A rattling old window is a major source of energy loss, but it can be rebuilt with inexpensive weatherstripping for a fraction of the cost of a new replacement window. When you shop for weatherstripping you'll discover there are many types on the market today. Traditionally spring brass weatherstripping was used to seal up double-hung windows. While it is very effective and long lasting, it is not easy to install. We found that adhesive-backed plastic (polypropylene) V-strip weatherstripping is much easier to install and almost as durable.

A roll of the V-strip seal costs under five dollars and in a half hour's time you can completely seal a window. You'll quickly recover the price of the weatherstripping and cut down your energy costs.

Before you replace worn weatherstripping, however, take the time to check for worn sash weights and any windows that stick and are difficult to open and fix these before proceeding.

If needed, pick up some sash cord and follow these simple directions.

Fixing a Worn Sash Weight

If you are faced with a stubborn window or want to replace broken sash cords then you will have to remove the inside stops and reinstall them later. Work carefully, removing the stops by using a stiff putty knife to protect the window jamb and a small pry bar or large screwdriver to remove the inner stop. Push the blade between the stop and jamb and gently pry up. If the stop is covered with many coats of paint, try to drive a putty knife between the stop and window jamb from the window track side of the stop. To prevent breaking the stop, pry only at the nail locations.

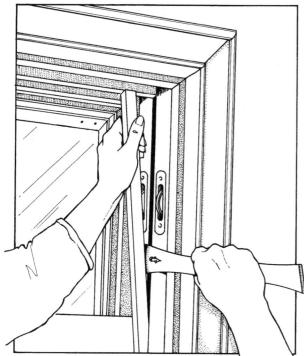

Use a small pry bar to gently remove the inner window stop.

The inner stops hold the window sash in place, so when they are removed be careful that the sash does not fall out. If the sash weight cords are broken or the window is very worn, the window will be loose in the jamb and may fall out of the jamb when you remove one of the stops. If the cords are still attached to the window, pull the sash out of the jamb and pry the cords out of their slots in the edge of the sash. The end of the sash cord may be held in place with a nail. If so, remove it. Then remove the window and set it aside in a safe place.

Remove the opening to the window weight compartment. Pull out the window weights and fill the cavity with insulation.

Lift out the access door to the weight compartment, which is located in the lower section of each side of the jamb. Some are held in place with screws, others with nails. Pull the sash weights out of the pockets and replace the worn sash weight cord with new rope. Use the old one as a model so you can tell how long to make the replacement. If the old cord broke or is missing, knot the end of the new cord and put it in the window sash like the old cord, then feed the other end through the pulley in the jamb and fish the end out of the weight pocket. Then raise the window all the way up and have someone hold it there while you tie the sash rope to the weight so the weight is several

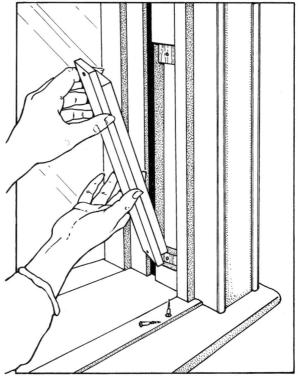

inches above the bottom of the weight compartment. Then lower the window and check that the rope is long enough to allow the window to fully close. Repeat this process on the other side of the window. Then replace the sash weight doors that cover up the pockets.

Weatherstripping the Sashes

The jambs of the window must be clean if you are using the self-adhesive type of weatherstripping. When applied on a clean jamb the adhesive has a good sound surface to stick to and the material will last two to five years, depending on how often you open and close the window. Wash the jamb carefully, especially the recesses where the sashes ride. Scrape away any loose paint and prime any bare wood spots before you install the weatherstripping.

Begin by lowering the outer sash and measuring its height. Cut two strips of weatherstripping about an inch longer than the sash. Install the V-strips close to the front of the window channel with the narrow end of the V pointing in. Peel off the paper backing from the bottom of the strip, fold it flat, and push it down between the outer sash and the jamb. Pull the top of the strip up flush with the top of the jamb and then remove the backing paper and press it in place. Do the same on the other side.

Raise the inner sash all the way and then pull the outer sash down to expose the meeting rail. Cut a piece of V-strip the width of the rail. Install it with the narrow end of the V pointing up. You may want to staple the adhesive flange to the sash with a heavy-duty stapler for additional security since this part of the weatherstripping takes a beating. Install another piece on the top of the outer sash with the narrow end of the V pointing in and then push the sash up to close it.

Cut strips of weatherstripping about one inch longer than the sash and install with the V pointing up along the width of the outer window sash.

The inner sash is sealed in the same way. Cut the weatherstripping slightly longer than the sash. It is installed with the narrow end of the V facing in. Push the sash all the way up to expose as much of the inner sash as possible.

The pressure-sensitive adhesive doesn't allow

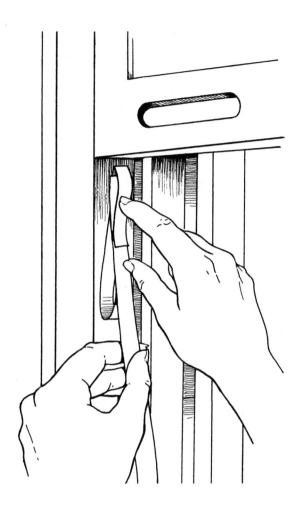

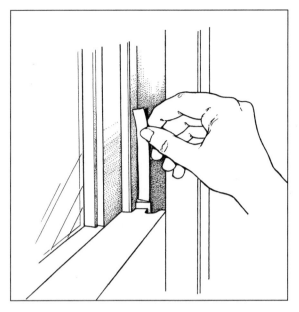

Above: Peel the backing paper from the upper part of the weatherstripping after you slide the inner sash down in place.

Left: Peel the paper back from the adhesive-backed weatherstripping and loop it over itself. Push the weatherstripping behind the inside sash and then press the lower section of weatherstripping in place.

you to slide the strips between the sash and jamb. To get around that problem try this trick. Take a piece of weatherstripping and cut the backing paper about a foot down from the top of the strip. Peel the paper back, working toward the top, so it doubles back on itself. Then fold a couple of inches of the backing over the top of the strip. This lets you push the weatherstripping up between the sash and jamb without the pressure-sensitive adhesive grabbing. Then peel the backing paper from the

lower part of the strip after you have aligned it flush with the bottom of the jamb. Press the material in place with your fingers.

Repeat this process on the other side and then lower the sash and pull the paper backing off the weatherstripping and stick it in place with your finger. Finish the job by applying a piece of weatherstripping to the bottom of the inner sash.

To reinstall the inner stop, reposition the nails in new holes or use longer nails in the existing holes so they will hold the stop firmly in place. Then recheck the window movement.

·Rebuild a Table·

Most homes have an old chair or table with a loose leg or a rung that has been reglued a few times but just refuses to stay put. There are many reasons this joint might keep loosening up, but probably the most likely reason is that the hole or mortise that the tenon fits into has been enlarged by the motion of the tenon every time the chair is used. This also happens with the legs of a table, and the more you use the table, the more wobbly it gets.

Permanent repair is not difficult when you use a standard steel corner brace, available at most large hardware stores or home centers. This corner brace is ideal for repairing loose chair and table legs.

Installation requires no special tools. Use a try square to true up the corner of the table or

Use a try square to draw guidelines on the inside face of the table sides.

chair frame and then measure 3 inches down each side and mark the saw kerf location. Use a try square to draw guidelines on the inside face of the table sides. Make shallow ⅛-inch-deep saw cuts along these layout lines. A ten-point crosscut saw works fine for this job.

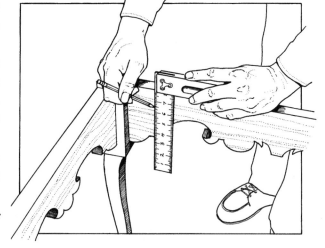

The brace is held to the sides of the table with a lag bolt. It is located in the edge of the leg at least a couple of inches from its top. Use a chisel to flatten the leg edge where you will drill the ¼-inch pilot hole for the lag bolt.

Drill the pilot hole for the lag bolt. Slide the steel plate into position, making sure its ends fit into the slots you cut in the table or chair sides, and then insert the lag bolt into the pilot hole in the leg and tighten it with an adjustable wrench.

Check that the corner is square and then tighten the screws that hold the brace against the sides and tighten the lag bolt. The tighter you make the nut, the more the steel plate pulls the joint together.

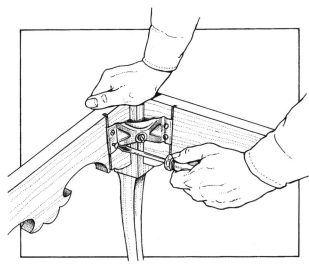

The steel corner brace is held to the table side with screws. Tightening the nut on the lag bolt pulls the joint together.

To refasten a loose table or chair rung, remove it from the chair or table and remove all old glue from the tenon and the mortise hole

with a chisel. Place the rung in a vise and make a thin saw cut through the tenon. Use a sharp chisel to chip off a sliver of wood from the edge of a piece of hardwood to make a small wedge.

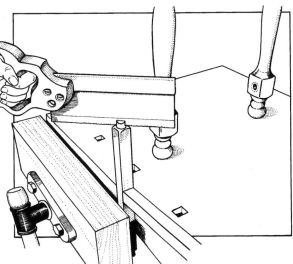

To refasten a loose joint, make a thin saw cut through the tenon and push a small wedge of wood into the slot to fill the gap.

Place the wedge in the saw kerf and push it into the slot as far as you can. Be careful not to break it off. Then trim the wedge to the width of the tenon and cut it off so that only about ⅛ inch protrudes from the end of the tenon.

Apply glue to the mortise and tenon and reassemble the chair or table. Drive the leg onto the rung, and as you do, the wedge will spread the tenon and make it tight in the mortise. Use a block of softwood to protect the leg from your mallet. Use a strap clamp to hold the joint overnight and allow the glue to dry.

If you don't have a strap clamp you can

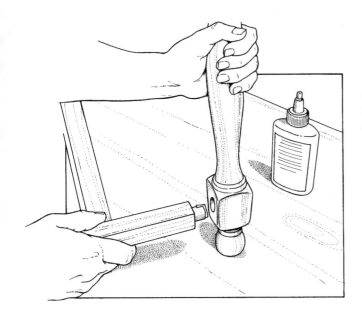

When assembling the legs, push the wedge into the tenon, spreading it so it fits tightly into the mortise.

make a tourniquet clamp to hold the legs together from a scrap of wood and some light rope or heavy twine. Wrap several loops of the rope around the legs and then tie the ends together. Slip the piece of scrap wood between the ropes, and then turn the wood to twist and tighten the rope. The more you turn the wood, the tighter the rope gets. Hold the piece of wood in place by tying it to a leg or one of the chair rungs until the glue is dry.

·Repair/Rehang Doors·

Over the years the doors in a house get a workout, and it's surprising that they operate in as trouble-free a manner as they do. They go virtually unnoticed until they don't work properly, and that's when some repair work is needed. Some of the most typical door problems relate to how they open and close, such as when a door sticks. Sometimes its latch doesn't work properly. Doors do wear out, but most of the time a faulty door can be repaired quite easily.

Determining just what is causing the problem can be the hardest part of the repair. Begin by making a close inspection of the door and its hardware to see that everything is in order. Many times a loose hinge screw or striker plate (into which the lock mechanism fits) is all that is wrong. Most of the time tightening screws solves the problem.

If you wait for the problem to become seri-ous it may be impossible to tighten loose screws because the screw holes have become enlarged by the constant movement of the loose screws as the door is opened and closed. If this is the case, tightening a loose hinge screw may provide temporary relief, but in a short time the screw will begin to loosen and cause trouble again.

To fix a loose screw, remove it, fill the hole with new wood, and then replace the screw. It's a simple matter of backing the screw out of the hole and then filling the hole with a wooden matchstick. Break the head of the match off and dispose of it safely; then dip the end of the matchstick in glue and push it into the screw hole. You can break the match off flush with the surface of the jamb by bending the match until it breaks off in the hole. You may want to put a second matchstick into the hole if it has been widened by the screw at the top of the hole.

You don't have to wait for the glue to dry to replace the screw. Simply force the tip of the screw into the hole and tighten it. The screw will compress the soft matchstick enough so that you don't need to drill a pilot hole. After the repair, close the door and leave it alone for an hour or so to allow the glue to set up.

This simple repair works well on light interior doors and cabinet doors, but matchsticks are made from softwood and are therefore not very effective at holding the large heavy loads imposed by exterior doors. To repair a loose

After enlarging the screw holes in a loose door hinge, coat a hardwood dowel with glue and drive it into the jamb. Drill pilot holes into the dowels and reinsert the screws.

screw in a hinge supporting this type of door you are better off removing all the screws from the hinge and swinging the hinge plate out of the mortise in the jamb. Then enlarge the hinge screw holes and glue hardwood dowels into the new holes.

Use $\frac{7}{16}$-inch diameter dowels for small hinges and $\frac{3}{8}$-inch holes for larger screws. Use a drill bit the same size as the dowel you are using to enlarge the screw hole in the jamb. Then push a piece of wire or even the drill bit into the hole and see how much space is left between the jamb and the wall framing. If possible, drill into the wall studs surrounding the doorjamb. Then cut the dowels long enough to go through the jamb and into the wall studs. Put glue into the hole in the jamb and on the ends of the dowels. Then insert them into the holes and tap the ends of the dowels with a hammer to drive them into the hole in the studs.

Allow the glue to dry and then cut the dowels off flush with the face of the hinge mortise. Replace the hinge leaf in the jamb mortise and use it as a template to mark the center of the hinge screw holes. Then drill a pilot hole for each hinge screw in the hardwood dowel. Insert the screws into the holes and tighten them, and your door is good as new. This repair will last and support heavy loads.

Sometimes a loose screw is not what causes a door to stick. If your door sticks at the top or bottom of the jamb, the hinge may be misaligned. If the door sticks at the bottom then readjustment of the top hinge may cure the problem. Of course the opposite is true if the door is sticking at the top.

To cure a door that rubs the jamb at the bottom but has ample clearance at the top, try this easy fix. Remove the screws from the jamb side of the top hinge. Then cut a piece of thin cardboard to fit into the jam mortise. Replace the hinge in the mortise and reinstall the screws. Use a large nail to poke a starting hole through the cardboard so you can thread the screws into the jamb. Tighten the screws securely.

Check the swing of the door. Adding a shim at the top will move the bottom of the door into alignment with the jamb. Of course, if your door was sticking at the top you would add a shim to the bottom hinge. Check the latch to be sure that the bolt catches in the striker plate on the doorjamb. If the latch bolt is far out of alignment with the striker plate you have to move the striker plate.

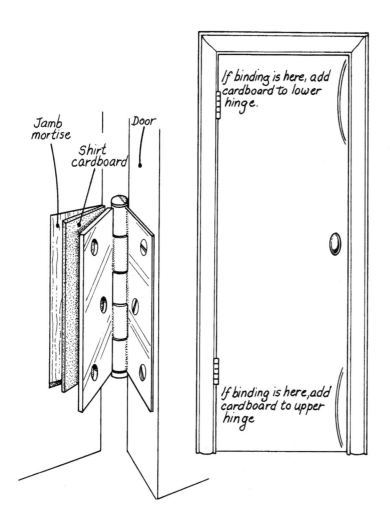

If a door binds or rubs at the top, remove the screws from the jamb of the bottom hinge and insert a thin piece of cardboard into the jamb mortise. For binding at the bottom of the door, put cardboard in the upper hinge.

Small adjustments can be made by filing the front edge of the striker plate until the latch bolt extends into the plate. If the bolt is high or low of the striker plate then you have to remove the plate and reinstall it. Fill the old screw holes with wood dowels and when the glue is dry reinstall the striker plate so it is in alignment with the latch bolt. You may have to enlarge the mortise that the striker plate is recessed into. Use a 1-inch chisel or one almost as wide as the striker plate to enlarge the mortise.

• PART THREE •

Woodworking Projects

•Colonial Candle Box•

A candle box was an essential home accessory during colonial times because it provided convenient storage for the only source of light. Today, an old-fashioned candle box is a charming reminder of days past and is used as a decorative piece to hold dried flowers, the mail, even candles.

   The simple design of this box makes it an ideal first-time woodworker's project. When building this project you'll get practice using a coping saw because the back piece has a graceful curve that is simple to follow. The construction of the box is

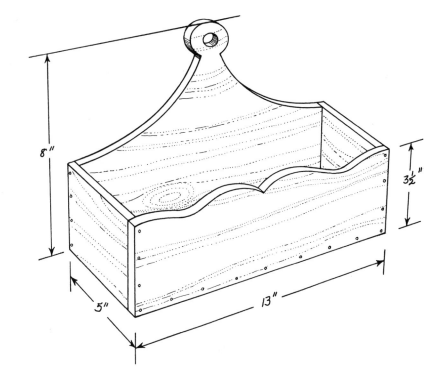

straightforward, with easy-to-construct butt joints.

Most large lumberyards carry ½-inch-thick pine. If your yard is the exception and does not stock it, ask them to plane ¾-inch stock down to size for you. There will probably be a small charge for this service.

You can finish the box with colorful paint or, for a more traditional look, use a wipe-on stain that's easy to apply.

How to Build It

Cut the front, side, and bottom pieces to length from the ½-inch stock. Unless your lumberyard carries unusually wide ½-inch lumber you will have to edge-glue two pieces together to make up the 8-inch-wide back piece.

Edge-gluing is not difficult. To get professional-looking results, apply glue to both edges

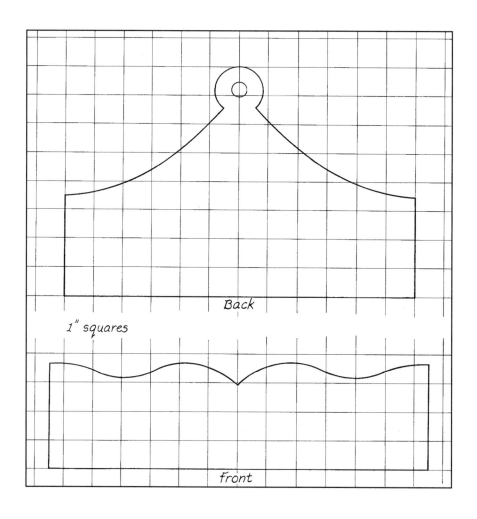

1" squares

Back

Front

of the boards and then place them on a flat surface. You don't have to worry about glue getting on your workbench because it can be scraped off later. If you are working on a table, protect the top with a piece of waxed paper placed under the joint where excess glue will ooze out when the pieces are clamped together.

You don't need much clamping pressure to join these boards. Use a web clamp, a set of bar clamps, or several thick rubber bands wrapped around the pieces. When you clamp the two pieces together make sure they stay flat while the glue dries.

After the glue has dried scrape off the excess with a sharp chisel. Then cut the glued-up piece of wood so that it is 8 inches wide. Then cut it to length.

Make a paper pattern from the grid patterns provided for the back and front parts. Then cut the patterns out and transfer the shapes to the boards. Use your coping saw to cut the curved edges of the back and front parts, keeping your saw cut outside the layout line. It can be challenging to cut a really fine line with a coping saw, so try this trick: cut close to the line but not along it, so you can go back with sandpaper and smooth the cut exactly to the shape you want. If you cut away the line you remove your guideline.

After you have cut the front and back parts, smooth all their edges with sandpaper. Use sandpaper wrapped around a sponge to sand the curved area. Because the sponge is pliable it adjusts well to curves. Then drill a ⅜-inch hole through the center of the top hanging loop of the back. Cut the side and bottom pieces to length.

Assembly is easy. First glue and nail the back to the bottom. Drive eight evenly spaced 1¼-inch wire brads through the bottom edge of the back about ¼ inch from the lower edge. Drive the brads through the back until their points just start to emerge from the front of the back piece. Then apply glue to the back edge of the bottom. Place the back on the bottom so it is flush at the bottom and ends. Then drive the brads all the way through to hold the parts together while the glue dries.

Next, glue and nail the sides to the back and bottom assembly. Apply glue to the edges of the back and bottom and then place the sides in position so they are flush with the back and bottom. Nail them in place with 1¼-inch wire brads. Then glue and nail the front to the sides and bottom.

Check that the box is square using a try square and set it aside to allow the glue to dry. After the glue has hardened use a nail set to sink the brad heads. Carefully remove any glue that has squeezed out of the joints with your chisel.

Finishing

Fill the nail head holes with wood putty and allow it to harden. Then sand the box with fine-grit sandpaper until it is smooth and clean it with a tack cloth to remove dust and grit. Then it is ready to paint or finish naturally.

If you want to paint the box, use a primer first and let it dry. Sand it lightly with a fine grit sandpaper and then finish with paint.

If you want a natural finish, sand the surface

smooth using a fine-grit sandpaper so all surfaces are the same. Choose a wipe-on gel finish such as the ones made by Barclays or tung oil by Minwax to coat the wood. Give the box a second application after lightly sanding the first coat.

TOOLS

Hammer	Drill with ⅜-inch bit
Nail set	Coping saw
Tape measure	Clamps
Chisel	Try square

PARTS LIST

Part		Number	Size	Material
A	back	1	½″ × 8″ × 12″	pine
B	front	1	½″ × 3½″ × 13″	pine
C	sides	2	½″ × 3½″ × 4½″	pine
D	bottom	1	½″ × 4″ × 12″	pine

MATERIALS LIST

Material	Amount	Size	Used For
pine	6 feet	½″ × 6″	all parts
carpenter's glue	1 small bottle		
wire brads	1 box	¼″	
120-grit sandpaper	2 sheets		
wood filler	1 small can		
tack cloth	1		

•Shaker Clock•

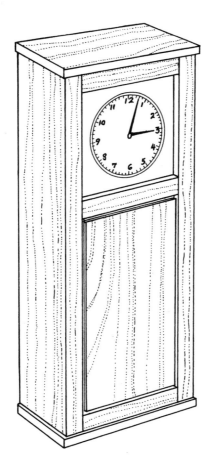

The simple yet classic lines of Shaker design are part of this wall clock. Its straight, unadorned style makes the clock a handsome addition to a room with just about any type of furnishings. We designed the clock using poplar, an inexpensive, easy-to-work-with wood that is readily available in most areas. Of course, this clock would be very attractive in cherry, oak, or almost any other hardwood.

This is probably the most challenging project in the book, but it's well worth the effort. The joinery has been simplified as much as possible. Butt joints and finish nails are used to assemble the clock case where traditionally a rabbeted joint would be used. We believe that having to fill a few small nail head holes is a small price to pay for an easier-to-build project.

The Shakers had to build the wood case and handcraft the clock movement. Today inexpensive but very accurate quartz clock movements are available through mail-order sources such as Klockit (see page 2 for mail-order information), so you can concentrate on the joinery. And a paper clock dial, also available through mail order, gives the clock a finished look.

How to Build It

The clock is composed of three main units: the clock case, the clock board assembly, and the door. Two remaining parts form the outer clock case and simply provide a solid top and a bottom on which to rest the clock.

Begin by making the clock case, as it is the easiest part of the project to build. It consists of a top, bottom, and sides. Cut these pieces to length from the one-by-eight stock. These parts are 6½ inches wide, so you will have to rip (cut lengthwise) off a ¾-inch strip from each piece. Be sure to leave the layout line visible on the wood; to do so cut on the waste side of your guidelines. Then after you have completed ripping these parts to the proper width, go back with your plane and dress up the edges of the boards.

Since it is difficult to cut a perfectly square edge with a handsaw, cabinetmakers "true up" a board with a bench plane. To do this, place the board you are truing on a flat surface with

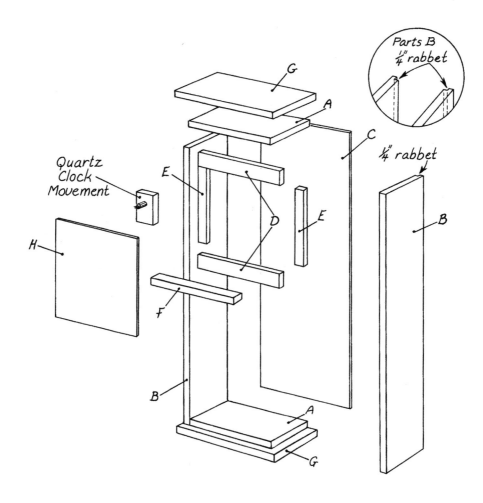

another piece of scrap under it to raise it up off the bench or table and then clamp it in place. Take a plane and place it on its side and plane the edge of the board. In this way the plane is held square to the edge of the board. Plane the rough wood down to the layout line but don't remove the line. (A woodworking jig called a shooting board makes this operation easy. Instructions for making a shooting board are on pages 134–37.) True up each clock case piece in turn.

The ¼-inch-thick plywood back piece is set into the case so its side edges are hidden. The top and bottom parts are cut ¼-inch narrower than the sides to provide a recess for the back. The sides must have a ⅜-inch-wide, ¼-inch-deep rabbet cut along their inside back edges to accept the back piece. A rabbet plane is designed to make this kind of cut since its cutter extends the full width of the plane so it can cut into a corner.

The clock case is easy to assemble. Apply glue to the ends of the top and bottom parts and then nail the sides to them with 4d finish

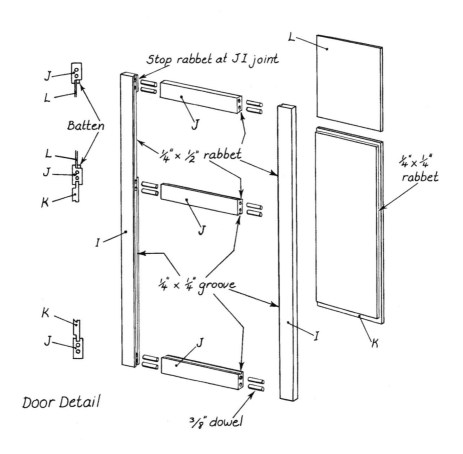

Door Detail

nails. Locate these nails ⅜ inch from the top and bottom of the side parts and drill a 1/16-inch pilot hole for all nails to prevent splitting the wood. If you don't have a small bit, cut the head off a finish nail and use it as a drill bit to make these holes. Note that the top and bottom case pieces are installed flush with the front edges of the sides and are set back ¼ inch at the rear.

Cut the back piece to size and test its fit in the back of the clock case. Use your plane to adjust it to size if necessary. Then tack it temporarily in place with a few 1-inch wire brads. You'll need to remove it later to add the clock mechanism and can then attach it securely.

Now you can begin cutting and installing the clock board assembly. The assembly is composed of a plywood square to which you attach a ready-made clock face, a narrow shelf on which the plywood square rests, and four cleats that support the plywood from the back. First, cut the cleats and the clock shelf to size, then

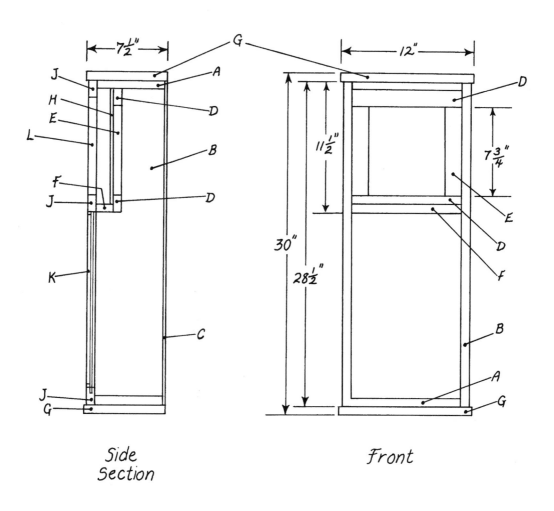

Side Section

Front

68

clean up the cut edges. The bottom cleat and the clock shelf that form the divider in the middle of the case are the same size as the cleat installed at the top of the case. Except for the front edge of the clock shelf, these pieces are not visible and may be made out of any type of wood. Cut these parts to size and then nail the bottom cleat to the back edge of the clock shelf to form an L. This assembly is installed in the clock case 11½ inches from the top of the case. Apply glue to the ends of this part and then insert it into the clock case and nail it in place with three 4d finish nails. Drive two nails through the side of the clock case into the ends of the shelf and one into the cleat.

Install the top and side cleats 1½ inches back from the front edge of the clock case or so they are flush with the bottom cleat and form a flat surface on which to place the plywood clock board. The board will be attached once the outer case top and bottom are attached.

Cut the two outer case parts, top and bot-

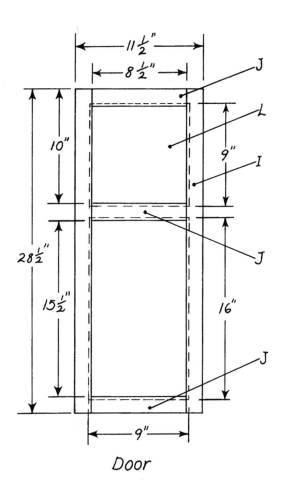

Door

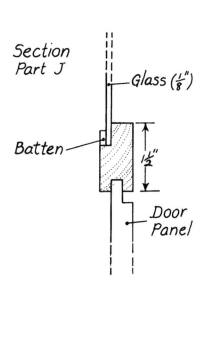

Section Part J

Glass ($\frac{1}{8}$")

Batten

$1\frac{1}{2}$"

Door Panel

tom, to size. These are nailed and glued to the outer top and bottom of the clock case. Apply glue to the ends of the sides and in the center of the top and then nail the outer case top in place with 4d finish nails. Drive the nails into the edge of the sides using two nails on each side. Install the outer case bottom in the same way.

While the glue used for the case assembly dries, cut the clock board to size from the ¼-inch plywood. Check that it is square by measuring the distance from the opposite corners. Then find the center by drawing a straight line from corner to corner. Mark the center of the clock board, which is at the intersection of these lines.

Drill a hole for the clock movement through this center mark. Many movements require a ⅜-inch hole. Check the installation instructions provided with the movement you've bought for specific dimensions. Then apply glue to the face of the cleats and put the clock board in place. Lay the whole clock on its back and put a heavy weight on the clock board while the glue dries.

Make the door next. The door frame is made from two long uprights called stiles and three shorter crosspieces called rails. A wood panel in the bottom portion and a glass panel in the top portion complete the door (with hinges, battens, and the doorknob to be added later).

Cut the rails and stiles to size and place them in position on a flat surface. Check the overall dimensions of the door assembly to see that the stiles are parallel and the rails are all the same size.

To mark the dowel location on both the stiles and rails at the same time, hold a try square against the edge of the stile so the blade extends across the stile into the rail.

Traditionally door rails and stiles are joined with mortised joints, but we chose to use dowel-reinforced joints instead. These are almost as strong and easier to make. Each joint is reinforced with two ⅜-inch dowels. While the stiles and rails are laid out flat, use your try square to mark the location of the dowels on both the stiles and rails together. Hold the body of the try square against the edge of the stile so the blade extends across the stile into the rail. This way you can mark the dowel locations on both parts with a single pencil line.

Then transfer the dowel layout lines from the faces of the parts to their ends. Take care to do this accurately. Place your dowel jig in alignment with these marks and drill a ⅜-inch diameter, 1-inch-deep hole for each dowel. Check the alignment as you go by placing mating parts next to one another on a flat surface. The dowel holes should be in alignment.

The panel in the bottom portion of the door fits into a ¼-inch-wide, ¼-inch-deep groove cut into the inside edges of the stiles and the bottom and center rails. The glass fits into a ¼-inch-wide, ½-inch-deep rabbet cut in the back of the center and top rails and the corresponding sections of the back of the stiles. To make the grooves in the stiles for the wooden panel, you will need a plane that can plow, or cut a groove. There are several multipurpose planes that are designed just for this operation. If you don't have such a plane, you can install the wood panel using the same size rabbet that you make for the glass panel.

If you do have a plane that can plow, set it up to cut a ¼-inch-wide, ¼-inch-deep groove in the center of the inside edges of the stiles, the top edge of the bottom rail, both edges of the center rail, and the lower edge of the upper rail. Plow the groove in the edges of the rail's full length. Plow the same size groove in the full length of the stiles, even though the end of the groove will be visible in the top edge of the finished door. The small notch can be filled with a scrap of wood after the door is fully assembled; this is easier than trying to stop the groove before you reach the end of the stile.

Make the rabbet for the glass by cutting away the inside edge of the groove on the top

rail and the upper inside edge of the center rail. Cut away the corresponding inside of the groove on the stiles. These edges surround the clock area. Use a fine-toothed (twelve-point) saw or a backsaw for this operation and then plane away any saw marks in the rabbet.

If you don't have a plane that can plow a groove, cut a ¼-inch-wide, ½-inch-deep rabbet along the inside back edge of the rails and stiles. You should cut this rabbet on the full length of the rails, but the rabbet on the stiles must stop wherever the rails and stiles meet. If you use this method, you'll need to secure the wood panel to the door frame with battens, as you will do later for the glass panel.

The door panel is made from ½-inch-thick wood. Plane a ½-inch-wide, ¼-inch-deep rabbet around its perimeter so it fits into the ¼-inch groove in the frame. When you are finished with the rabbet, check the fit of the panel in the grooves in the rails and stiles. The panel should have a snug, but not tight, fit. Bet-

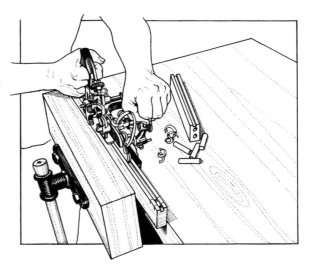

Use a Multiplane setup to make the door and glass panel groove. Cut these grooves full length on all parts, then fill the small gap at the top and bottom of the door joint with wood blocks.

ter a little loose than too tight because the wood might expand or shrink slightly with changes in humidity.

If you can't find ½-inch-thick wood at your lumberyard, make the panel out of ¾-inch stock and cut a ½-inch-wide, ¼-inch-deep rabbet on both sides of the panel. Cutting a rabbet on each side forms a ¼-inch-thick, ½-inch-wide tongue that will fit into the groove you made in the rails and stiles.

Now you can assemble the door frame. The wood panel is installed as the door is assembled, and the glass panel is added after the frame is completed. In this way, if the glass ever breaks, you can easily replace it without disassembling the door. First apply glue to the ends of the rails and put a little glue in each dowel hole and in the mating holes in the stile. Then tap the dowels into the holes in the sides of the stiles. Install the rails by pushing them down on the dowels protruding from the stiles. You may have to tap the end of the rails to fully seat them on the dowels. Don't hit the end of the rail directly; place a piece of scrap between it and your hammer to protect it.

Clean out any glue from the groove in the stiles and insert the door panel. Check that its face is oriented toward the front of the door. Then apply glue to the ends of the rails and put a little glue into the dowel holes and insert the dowels into the holes in the rails. Then put the stiles in place, aligning the dowels with the holes in the stiles.

When everything is together, place the assembly on a flat surface and apply a clamp at each junction between the top, middle, and bottom rails and the stiles. Use a try square to check that the door is square and then allow the glue to dry.

After the glue is dry, remove any excess that might have squeezed out of the joints with a sharp chisel. Drive the few finish nail heads in the clock case below the wood surface with your nail set and then fill the small holes with wood putty.

The wood doorknob is located in the center of the door rail and aligned with the center stile. Drill a ⅛-inch hole for the mounting screw. Place the screw into the hole and thread on the knob until it is drawn down tight against the door rail.

Then give the clock case and door a careful sanding. Pay special attention to the exposed end grain, which is more porous. It will absorb more stain and look darker if you don't carefully sand it. After sanding, carefully dust the clock case and door and use a tack cloth to remove any grit, then apply a finishing stain.

When the finish is dry, insert the glass into the upper opening of the door and hold it in place with the battens. Tack the battens in place with ¾-inch wire brads. Install the door on the clock face with two 2½-inch brass hinges. The no-mortise-type hinge that folds back into itself is a good choice because it does not require a mortise in the clock case or door. Place the hinges 2 inches from the top and bottom of the clock case. If you use standard hinges use them as templates to mark the mortise location on the edge of the clock frame and back of the door.

Glue the clock face to the clock board and then insert the shaft of the quartz movement through the hole in the center of the clock board and secure it with the nut and washers provided. Then install the hands on the movement shafts. If you purchased a clock movement with a pendulum, install it after the clock is on the wall or in its permanent location.

Nail the back in place with ¾-inch wire brads spaced about 4 inches apart.

TOOLS

Measuring tape	½″ wood chisel
Try square	Hand drill and bits
Hammer	Brace and ⅜″ bit
Nail set	Rabbet plane
Crosscut saw (ten-point or finer)	Bench plane
Miter box and backsaw	Shooting board

PARTS LIST

	Part	*Number*	*Size*	*Material*
A	top/bottom	2	¾″ × 6¼″ × 10″	pine
B	side	2	¾″ × 6½″ × 28½″	pine
C	back	1	¼″ × 11″ × 28½″	plywood
D	top/mid cleats	2	¾″ × 1½″ × 10	pine
E	side cleats	2	¾″ × 1½″ × 7¾″	pine
F	clock shelf	1	¾″ × 1½″ × 10	pine
G	outer case	2	¾″ × 7½″ × 12″	pine
H	clock board	1	¼″ × 10″ × 10″	plywood
I	door stile	2	¾″ × 1½″ × 28½″	pine
J	door rail	3	¾″ × 1½″ × 8½″	pine
K	door panel	1	½″ × 9″ × 16″	pine
L	door glass	1	⅛″ × 9″ × 9″	glass
M	battens	4	¼″ × ¼″ × 9″	pine (cut from scrap)

MATERIALS LIST

Material	Amount	Size	Used For
1″ × 2″ pine board	1	12 foot	cleats/door
1″ × 8″ pine board	1	8 foot	clock case
1″ × 12″ pine board	1	3 foot	outer case
plywood	¼ sheet	¼″	back/clock board
plate glass	1	9″ × 9″	clock window
no-mortise brass hinges	2	2½″	
finish nails	1 box	4d	
wire brads	1 box	¾″	
carpenter's glue	1 small bottle		
paper dial (Klockit #B26088K)	1	10″ × 10″	
quartz clock movement (Klockit #10002K)	1	¼″-thick dial	
Shaker-style knob	1	small	
120-grit sandpaper	2 sheets		
hardwood dowels	12	2″ long, ⅜″ diameter	

·Picture Frames·

Have you ever wanted to frame a favorite picture, poster, or photograph only to find out it would cost a small fortune? In some cases the frame can actually cost more than the artwork. You can sidestep the custom framework and make your own with hand tools by using moldings found at lumberyards and home centers.

Just about any molding can be used, but some lend themselves to framing better than others. Moldings like ply cap, which is designed to fit over another piece of wood, have a rabbet cut in their back side that provides a recess in which to place the artwork. Other moldings, like picture and rake moldings, have a flat back that can be glued to a piece of lattice or parting bead to form a recess for your picture. With a little bit of imagination just about any style of molding can be used.

To make a picture frame you need a miter box to cut the 45-degree angles that form the

mitered joints at the four corners and a web or strap clamp to hold the frame together while the glue dries. To guarantee a tight joint we suggest that you use the miter shooting board described on pages 136–37 so you can trim up the cuts with a plane and produce a perfect fit even when your sawing is a little off.

How to Build It

Whatever molding you decide to use, the basic construction of your picture frame is the same. If you are using a piece of molding without a cut in its back side then you have to glue a piece of lattice or parting bead to the back of the molding. Use lattice that is ¼ inch thick if you are not using a piece of glass or a thick mat or heavy cardboard back. Otherwise use two

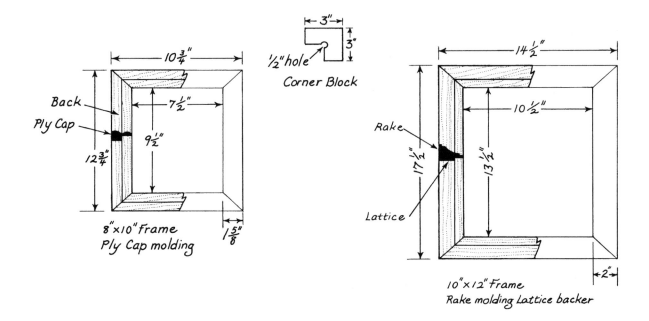

Back
Ply Cap

$10\frac{3}{4}"$

$7\frac{1}{2}"$

$9\frac{1}{2}"$

$12\frac{3}{4}"$

$8"\times10"$ Frame
Ply Cap molding

$1\frac{5}{8}"$

$3"$
$3"$
$\frac{1}{2}"$ hole
Corner Block

$14\frac{1}{2}"$

$10\frac{1}{2}"$

Rake

$17\frac{1}{2}"$

$13\frac{1}{2}"$

Lattice

$2"$

$10"\times12"$ Frame
Rake molding Lattice backer

pieces of lattice or parting bead that is ½-inch thick to provide room for the glass-and-mat sandwich.

Apply glue to the parting stop or lattice and then place it on the back of the molding. Align it flush with the back edge of the molding. You can hold it in place while the glue dries with wire brads driven through the lattice or parting bead into the back of the molding, which doesn't harm the front or face of the molding. After the glue is dry, use a sharp chisel to remove any glue that has been squeezed out of the joint.

Before cutting the molding to length, apply an undercoat of primer or the first coat of finish, but wait until it is assembled to apply the topcoat. The last coat covers any small imperfections or areas where your saw or plane might have nicked the undercoat.

The end of each piece of the frame has a 45-degree angle cut in it to form the miter joint. It is easiest to measure from the point of the angle or along the long side of the piece. Since you are dealing with 45-degree angles, the inside or short edge of the piece will be shorter than the longer edge by the width of the part. If the molding is 2 inches deep, the long edge of the frame will be 2 inches longer than the short edge at each end. Therefore the longer edge of each side of the picture frame will be longer than the shorter edge by twice the width of the frame. For example, if the short edge of a 2-inch-wide piece measures 10 inches, then the long edge will be 14 inches.

Lay out and cut the miter angles using the long dimension. If you are using the miter shooting board, add about ⅛ inch to the overall length to allow for trimming. Just be sure you cut well outside the layout marks and then trim the piece back to these marks with your plane

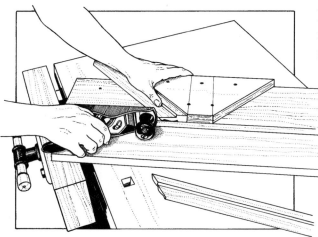

Make all saw cuts outside the layout lines, then use the miter shooting board and a plane to true up all the angles of your frame.

large enough so the corner of your frame does not come in contact with the block. The hole in the block allows the block to force the frame together at the corners.

Apply glue to the joints of the frame, clamp it together on a flat surface, and allow the glue to dry overnight. Wipe away any excess glue from the face of the frame with a damp rag before it hardens. It is easier to wipe glue away at this point rather than try to chip it out of the curved recesses of the molding after it is hard. Remove any excess glue from the back of the frame with your chisel.

When the glue is dry, apply the final coat of finish and you are ready to insert the artwork into the frame. Wire brads driven into the inside edge of the frame flush against the backing will hold the glass, artwork, matting, and cardboard back securely in the frame. Place them 3 to 4 inches apart around the perimeter of the frame. Check the front for any dirt or dust and to see that everything is clean and properly aligned. Then seal the back of the frame with brown wrapping paper by running a bead of glue around the back of the frame and applying the paper to it. Allow it to set for a couple of minutes and then trim away the excess paper with a sharp razor or utility knife.

and shooting board. Make sure that the opposite sides of your picture frame are exactly the same length or the frame will be out of square and the joints will not fit together.

Clamping the frame together can be a bit of a challenge, but a simple web clamp and four corner blocks will hold most frames together while the glue dries. Cut the corner blocks from scrap stock and use any size that fits the frame; ¾ inch or greater is best. The size is not too important as long as they cover the corner and the relief hole in the corner of the block is

TOOLS

Measuring tape	Plane
Try square	Miter shooting board
Miter box and backsaw	⅜″ or ½″ wood chisel
	Utility knife

PARTS LIST

*To make one frame for 8″ × 10″ artwork
using 1⅝″-wide ply cap molding*

Part	Number	Size	Material
Top/bottom	2	10¾″ long	pine ply cap molding
Side	2	12¾″ long	pine ply cap molding

*To make one frame for 11″ × 14″ artwork
using 2″-wide rake molding*

Part	Number	Size	Material
Top/bottom	2	14½″ long	rake molding
Backer	4	¼″ × 1⅝″ × 14½″	lattice
Side	2	17½″ long	rake molding
Backer	4	¼″ × 1⅝″ × 17½″	lattice

MATERIALS LIST

Material	Amount	Size	Used For
1⅝″ ply cap molding	1	6 foot	top/bottom side
2″ picture molding	1	8 foot	top/bottom side
1⅝″ lattice	2	14 foot	top/bottom side backer
carpenter's glue	1 small bottle		
wire brads	1 box	¾″	
120-grit sandpaper	2 sheets		
brown backing paper (use as needed)	1 sheet		

•Wall Dish Shelf•

Show off a collection of plates in this easy-to-build pine dish shelf. Whether it is showcasing stoneware or porcelain, this shelf is a good-looking wall decoration for anywhere in the house. It measures 5½ inches deep at the top with a 2½-inch shelf that holds at least three 9-inch-diameter plates. You can customize the length of this shelf to accommodate the number of plates in your collection.

The wall shelf is made of only ten pieces of wood and uses readily available lumber. All of the major parts are cut from a single one-by-six board. The back is made by edge-gluing two pieces together. The decorative lip on the top is formed by a piece of cove molding. Of course, if you have a molding plane this edge can be cut into the edge of the top.

A groove in the bottom shelf holds your decorative plates in an upright position, and a batten runs across the shelf connecting the two ends. The top shelf and sides provide protection from dust.

How to Build It

This project is basically built from dimensional lumber so no ripping is required. Shaping the sides is probably the most challenging job so there's a simple pattern provided. Transfer the shape of the pattern to a piece of one-by-six and then use a coping saw to cut the front edge contour. When you have one side cut out, use it as a pattern to make the other. The exact shape is not critical as long as the top measures 5½ inches and the bottom measures 3¼ inches. When these parts are cut out use clamps to hold them together and sand the front edges of both parts so they match. For the best-looking results make sure the parts are identical. To sand the curved areas, wrap sandpaper around a sponge so you can smooth all the surfaces, not just the flat ones. Because the sponge is pliable and adjusts to any contour, it lets you sand all the areas smoothly.

When the sides are completed cut the back, top, and shelf to length. Make these cuts carefully so the ends of the pieces are square. Make your cut on the waste side of the layout line and leave it visible. When you are finished go back with your plane and square up the board ends.

There is a groove cut ¼ inch back from the front edge of the shelf to hold the edges of the plates. We found that a ⅜-inch-wide groove fit our plates, or you can make the groove ½-inch wide. Do some experimenting with your plates to decide the groove width needed. If you have a plane that makes a dado, then creating the groove is easy; it can also be made with a saw and chisel. Lay out the location of the groove on the shelf with two lines, one on either side of the layout line. Then make a ¼-inch-deep saw cut along the inside of the layout line and use a chisel to remove the wood between the saw kerfs. If you are making a ½-inch-wide groove make several more saw cuts inside the two you just made. These additional saw kerfs will help you maintain a constant depth as you chisel out the excess wood.

To begin assembling the project, glue and

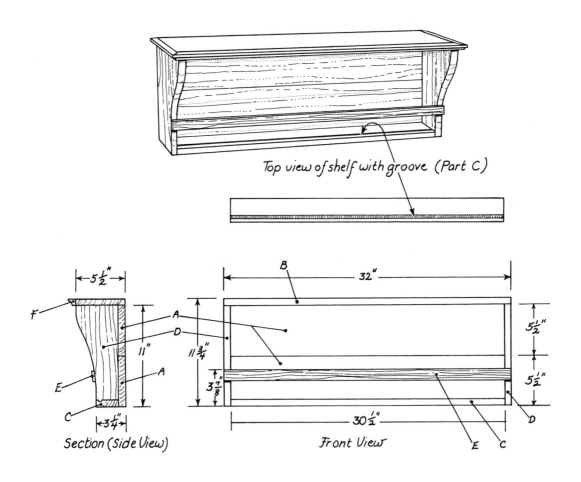

Top view of shelf with groove (Part C)

Section (Side View)   Front View

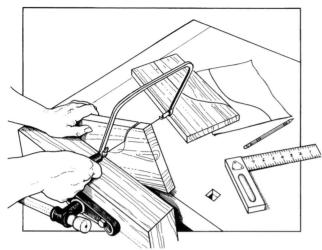

Use a coping saw to cut the front edge contour of the ends. Then clamp the parts together and smooth with sandpaper to make a matched pair.

nail the shelf to one of the back boards. Use 6d finish nails and drive six nails, evenly spaced, through the back of the back board about ⅜ inch up from its bottom edge. Drive the nails in until their points just start to emerge from the face of the back. Apply glue to the back edge (opposite side from groove) and then along it so it is flush with the bottom edge of the back. Check that the ends are aligned and then drive the nails home (through the wood so the heads are flush with the surface of the back piece).

The sides are installed next. Drive a few evenly spaced nails through the bottom outside face of one side piece ⅜ inch from its bottom. Then drive eight nails, evenly spaced, ⅜ inch from its back. Drive these 6d finish nails just deep enough so their tips emerge from the other side. Then apply glue to the ends of the back and shelf assembly. Carefully align it flush

with the bottom and back edge of the side piece and drive the nails home. Apply glue to the remaining back board and install it in the same way, with glue and 6d finish nails.

Flip the unit over and install the other side piece in the same way. Then apply glue to the top of the side pieces and along the top edge of the back board and install the top. Set the unit aside to allow the glue to dry.

Cut the cove molding to fit the top. See "Trim Out a Room with Ceiling Molding" on pages 36–41 to read about making mitered cuts. Begin at one end and cut and fit the piece. Tack it in place with 3d finish nails but don't drive the nails home or use any glue. Next cut and fit the front piece of cove molding and then the other end piece. When you are satisfied with the fit of the pieces of molding, remove them and apply glue. Then install them permanently. To install the batten, apply glue to its ends and nail it across the front of the side pieces about 2¾ inches from the bottom.

Use a nail set to sink all nail heads below the wood surface and then fill the depressions with wood filler. Use a sharp chisel to remove any hardened glue that squeezed out of the joints during assembly. After the wood filler has hardened, sand it smooth and give the entire shelf unit a careful sanding. Don't forget to sand the batten.

For a colorful pastel finish choose one of the wipe-on finishes that create a whitewashed look. Pastels by Minwax is a good one. You can paint the dish shelf in a gloss enamel paint or, for a more traditional look, choose a light stain to bring out the texture of the wood. If using a stain, first use a wood conditioner to prevent the stain from blotching, then apply the stain.

TOOLS

Measuring tape   Coping saw
Try square   Miter box and backsaw
Hammer   Plane
Nail set $\frac{3}{8}''$ or $\frac{1}{2}''$ wood chisel
Crosscut saw

PARTS LIST

Part	Number	Size	Material
A back	2	$\frac{3}{4}'' \times 5\frac{1}{2}'' \times 30\frac{1}{2}''$	pine
B top	1	$\frac{3}{4}'' \times 5\frac{1}{2}'' \times 32''$	pine
C shelf	1	$\frac{3}{4}'' \times 2\frac{1}{2}'' \times 30\frac{1}{2}''$	pine
D side	2	$\frac{3}{4}'' \times 5\frac{1}{2}'' \times 11''$	pine
E batten	1	$\frac{1}{4}'' \times 1\frac{1}{8}'' \times 32''$	pine
F front molding	1	$\frac{3}{4}'' \times \frac{3}{4}'' \times 33\frac{1}{2}''$	pine
G side molding	2	$\frac{3}{4}'' \times \frac{3}{4}'' \times 6\frac{1}{2}''$	pine

MATERIALS LIST

Material	Amount	Size	Used For
$1'' \times 6''$	1	10 foot	back/top/end
$1'' \times 3''$	1	3 foot	shelf
$\frac{3}{4}''$ cove	1	6 foot	molding
finish nails	1 box	6d	
finish nails	1 box	3d	
carpenter's glue	1 small bottle		
120-grit sandpaper	2 sheets		

· Serving Tray ·

Some wooden trays are lovely to look at but not too practical because beverage glasses slip and slide on their surfaces. This tray, however, is lined with cork to provide a surefooted surface that is ideal for carrying glasses. Cutout handles make it convenient to grip while serving even a trayful of heavy glassware.

You'll find that building the tray is straightforward, from cutting out the pieces to final assembly. Come Christmastime you might find this project is a good choice for gift-giving and decide to make more than one of these handy servers.

How to Build It

This project can be built using scrap pieces of wood that you'll find in most lumberyards.

They have a bin where they throw pieces of wood from the cut-off sections of longer boards. In these bins you can usually find small pieces of plywood or dimensional lumber priced inexpensively. You may also find some hardwoods in this pile.

To build the serving tray we used one-by-four pine for the ends and 1⅜-inch lattice for the sides, but you can use a hardwood like maple, birch, or mahogany. Use a piece of plywood for the bottom because it is more dimensionally stable than individual boards.

Begin building the tray by cutting the end, side, and bottom pieces to size. The location for the top curve of the handhold in the end pieces is shown in the grid below. The easiest way to make the cutout is to drill two 1¼-inch holes and then cut away the wood between the holes with a saw. The centers of the holes are located 1⅝ inches from the bottom edge of the

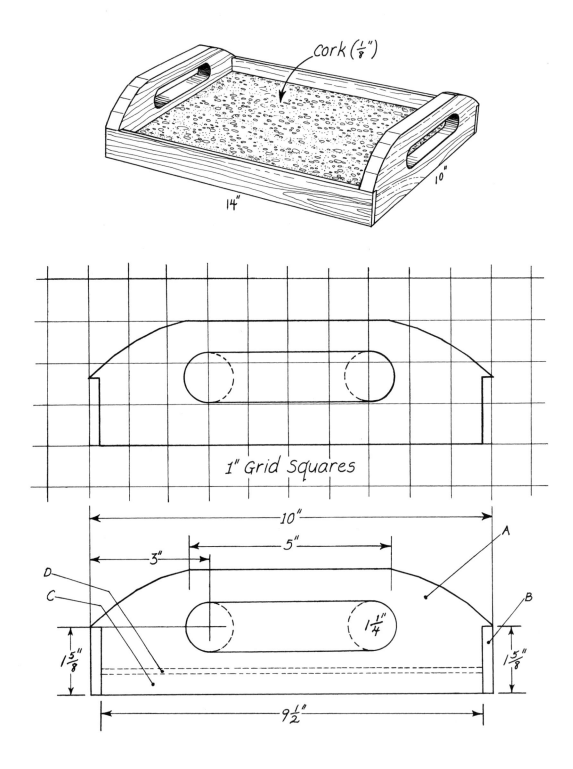

cork ($\frac{1}{8}$")

10"

14"

1" Grid Squares

10"

5"

3"

A

D

C

B

$1\frac{1}{4}$"

$1\frac{5}{8}$"

$1\frac{5}{8}$"

$9\frac{1}{2}$"

end and 3 inches from its end. Lay out these points and then drill the holes with your brace and bit. Place the parts on top of a piece of scrap lumber to protect your workbench from the point of the bit. To prevent the bit from tearing the wood as it exits the hole, turn the part over as soon as the point of the bit emerges from the back side of the wood and finish the holes from the opposite side. Then connect the holes with straight pencil lines and cut along the lines with a coping or keyhole saw to form the handhold slot.

Cut the recesses for the sides in the ends of the end parts. These notches are basically the same dimension as the sides. The lattice is ¼ inch thick by 1⅝ inches high, so lay out the notches on the ends. Mark both sides of these parts to help you cut straight and square since you will then have a guideline on both sides of the part to follow. Remember to make your cut on the waste side of the layout lines so the lines remain on the part. Then go back with a chisel or a block of wood wrapped with sandpaper and clean up the notch. Test-fit the side parts in the notch and adjust them for a snug fit.

Use a coping saw to cut the curves along the tops of the two end parts. Then clamp both of the parts together and sand away the saw marks from both of them at the same time. Working on them together assures that they will be the same size and shape. Smooth the inside of the handhold and the sharp edges along the top thoroughly with a sanding block. For tight spaces use a short scrap of dowel wrapped in sandpaper or a strip of sandpaper on the back of a piece of masking tape. Use the strip like den-

Use a brace fitted with a 1 ¼-inch bit to drill holes at each end of the handhold, then cut away the wood between them with a coping saw.

tal floss, working back and forth in a steady manner.

Cut a piece of rolled sheet cork slightly larger than the bottom part. Then spread carpenter's glue on the bottom and place the cork on it. Pile some heavy weights (books or bricks) on the plywood bottom and cork to hold them flat until the glue dries. Then trim the cork flush with the edges of the bottom using a utility knife.

To assemble the tray, first drive six evenly spaced 4d finish nails along the bottom edges of the end parts. Drive these nails through the wood until their points begin to emerge from the other side. Place the nails ¼ inch from the bottom. Then apply glue to the end of the bottom. Position an end part on the edge with glue so it is aligned and flush with the bottom of the end. Also check that the bottom is flush with the sides of the notches. Then drive the nail home, being careful not to damage the face (outer surface) of the wood with your hammer. Install the other end in the same way.

Apply glue to the edge of the bottom and into the notches. Then place the side in position and check that it is flush at both ends with the outside face of the end. Then nail it in place with 1-inch wire brads. Install the other side in the same way.

After the glue has hardened use a sharp chisel to chip away any excess glue that has squeezed out of the joints. Use a nail set to sink the nail heads below the surface of the wood and then fill the depressions with wood filler and allow it to harden.

Give the tray a complete sanding with 120-grit sandpaper followed by 220-grit paper. Pay special attention to the end grain of the sides and ends.

You can finish the tray naturally using tung oil, which is easy to apply with a rag and will protect the wood surfaces. Build up this top-coat protection with several applications. Avoid getting oil on the cork by running masking tape around its edges to protect it.

TOOLS

Measuring tape	Coping saw
Try square	Brace and $1\frac{1}{8}''$ bit
Hammer	$\frac{3}{8}''$ or $\frac{1}{2}''$ wood chisel
Nail set	Utility knife
Crosscut saw	

PARTS LIST

	Part	Number	Size	Material
A	end	2	$\frac{3}{4}'' \times 3'' \times 10''$	pine
B	side	2	$\frac{1}{4}'' \times 1\frac{5}{8}'' \times 14''$	pine
C	bottom	1	$\frac{1}{2}'' \times 9\frac{1}{2}'' \times 12\frac{1}{2}''$	plywood
D	cork liner	1	$\frac{1}{2}'' \times 9\frac{1}{2}'' \times 12\frac{1}{2}''$	sheet cork

MATERIALS LIST

Material	Amount	Size	Used For
pine	2 feet	1″ × 4″	end
lattice	3 feet	1⅝″	side
plywood	scrap	½″	bottom
cork	12″ × 24″ sheet	⅛″	cork liner
finish nails	1 box	4d	
wire brads	1 box	1″	
carpenter's glue	1 small bottle		
120-grit sandpaper	2 sheets		
220-grit sandpaper	2 sheets		
masking tape			

·Knife Block·

This knife block is designed to look good sitting on a kitchen counter while it serves as a safe storage area for cutlery. It is tall enough to accommodate large knives, but it is slanted so it fits under wall-hung kitchen cabinets and provides easy access to the knives.

The block is made of twenty layers of wood laminated together in four basic units. Each unit is made of two side pieces with three spacers sandwiched between. The construction begins with cutting out the individual layers and then aligning and laminating them.

How to Build It

This is the type of project that is great for using up wood scraps around the shop. Common one-by-eight pine and pine lattice are specified,

but there is no reason you can't use smaller pieces and glue them together. Since only the outside boards are visible you can use wood with knots and other defects for the center laminates. For a more contemporary look with contrasting shades of wood, substitute strips of hardboard or other dark-colored wood for the pine lattice.

Construction is very easy, but be careful cutting the ends of each laminate; they should be as square as possible. And try to make the angled cut across the top as uniform as possible. First cut the one-by-eight pine that forms the eight main laminate parts. Cut them to length and then lay out the angled cut. To mark the layout line, first measure 8 inches up from the bottom of the part and make a pencil mark on the edge. Then connect this mark with the opposite top corner.

Clamp a piece of straight scrap along the

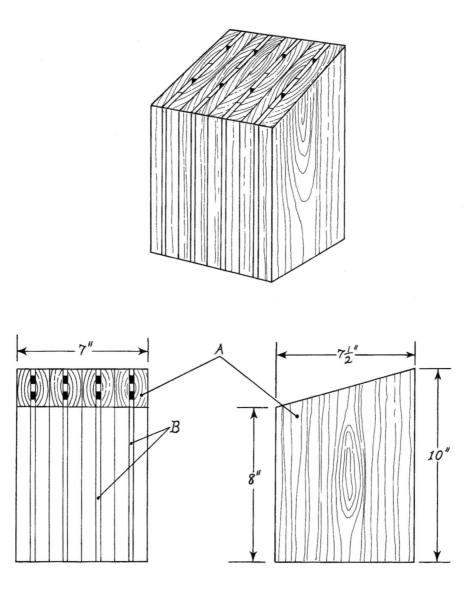

layout line to help guide your saw when you make the angled cut. You can then clamp the first part to the piece you are cutting and use it as a guide. This will help guarantee that all the laminates are the same size.

The twelve spacers are arranged to suit your particular knives, but there must be one flush at the front and flush at the back of the block between each pair of laminates. To find the best spacing for your knives, cut all the parts to one length and then place one of the laminate parts on a flat surface. Place the spacers at the front and back and then place a knife on the board. Put the long knives toward the top, where the block is tallest. Usually two knives per compartment works best. You can trim the spacers to the exact size required after you are sure of their placement.

Place two laminate parts on the assembly and leave the knives in place. Put your next set of knives in place and repeat this process until you have all your knives in the block and the outer side is in place. Check the fit of your knives, removing them and inserting them a few times. If their handles conflict, disassemble the block and reposition the knives.

When you are satisfied with the knife placement, take the block apart and as you do, mark the parts with a light pencil mark so they can be reassembled in the correct order.

Assembling the knife block with glue can get a bit messy, so work on a sheet of plastic (or a garbage bag) to prevent the glue from getting all over your work area. Start with one of the

end pieces and glue the spacers to it, following your pencil marks. Use a few 1-inch wire brads to hold the spacers in place and then recheck their alignment. Check the placement of the outer spacers carefully as you assemble the block; small protrusions can be sanded or planed down, but if the spacers are recessed behind the middle layers, a depression will be formed. The only way to remove this depression is to grind down the entire side of the block.

Apply glue to the assembled spacers and place a laminate on top of them. Align it carefully and then hold them in place with several 4d finish nails. Be very careful to drive these nails so they penetrate the spacers and are not between them, blocking the knife slot. Follow the same process for the remaining layers.

After you have completed the assembly, set the block upright and allow the glue to dry. It is easier and more effective to chip away the excess glue after it has dried rather than trying to wipe it off while it's still tacky because you end up spreading the glue around while wiping it. Use a sharp chisel to remove any excess hardened glue that might have squeezed out of the joints. Test the fit of your knives, and if any glue has spread into the knife slot, chip it away with the knife blade. Then trim the top and bottom of the spacers to fit the rest of the block.

Sand the block smooth with 120-grit sandpaper wrapped around a piece of wood or use a sanding block. Round all sharp corners with the

Use 1-inch wire brads and glue to assemble the layers of the sides and spacers. Check that the spacers are flush at the ends and sides of the unit.

sanding block, giving the top of the block special attention. The end grain of the wood must be very smooth or it will take the finish unevenly.

You can find nontoxic wood finishes for salad bowls and butcher-block countertops in specialty woodworking catalogs. We prefer using mineral oil as a natural finish. Soak a rag in mineral oil and use it to wipe the block. Let one application soak into the wood and dry for a couple of hours before applying a second coat. When the knife block gets dirty, sand it and reapply a few coats of mineral oil.

TOOLS

Hammer	Crosscut saw
Measuring tape	½″ wood chisel
Try square	Sanding block

PARTS LIST

Part		Number	Size	Material
A	side	8	¾″ × 7½″ × 10″	pine
B	spacer	12	¼″ × 1⅛″ × 12″	lattice

MATERIALS LIST

Material	Amount	Size	Used For
1″ × 8″ common pine	2	8 foot	sides
1⅛″ pine lattice	1	12 foot	spacers
carpenter's glue	1 small bottle		
finish nails	1 box	4d	
120-grit sandpaper	4 sheets		

· Bench with Storage ·

You'll find more than one spot in your house for this bench because of its handy concealed storage compartment. The storage area is reached by raising the seat of the bench, which is actually a lid hinged on one side to open and close. In a mudroom the bench is perfect for taking off boots or messy shoes and for storing hats and gloves. Used in a bedroom or family room, the bench can stow away needlework and act as a footstool. It's a versatile piece of furniture you'll find many uses for.

The bench is made of pine and consists of six pieces cut to size and then assembled.

How to Build It

When designing this project we paid more attention to making the bench attractive than to making it as easy to build as possible. The ends and sides require special attention to sawing and shaping, but we feel the finished result is well worth the effort.

The ends require the most work, so begin with them first. Making the semicircle at the bottom of the end is easier if you cut both end parts at the same time. All you have to do is lay out a circle in the center of the board, cut it out, and then cut the board in half to create the parts.

First cut a piece of one-by-twelve lumber to 36 inches (the total length of both ends). Then use a try square to draw a straight pencil line across the board 18 inches from either end. Mark the center of this line, which is located $5\frac{5}{8}$ inches from the edge of the board. Use this point as the center and draw a circle with a $3\frac{5}{8}$-inch radius. You can use a compass or tie a piece of string around the pencil and use it as a compass.

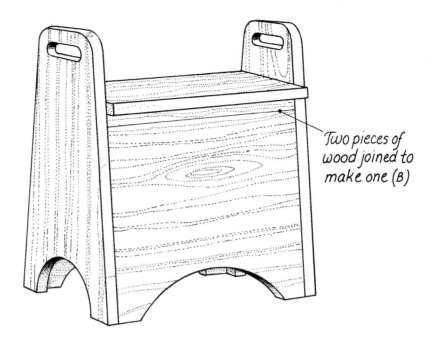

Two pieces of wood joined to make one (B)

Drill a ½-inch-diameter hole inside the circle near its circumference. Then use your coping saw to cut along the circular layout line and remove the circle. Cut this piece of wood in half along the center line to form the two legs on either end piece.

The top of the ends are tapered to 7 inches. Make a pencil mark at the center of the board (5⅝ inches from the edge). Then measure in from the outer corner 2⅛ inches and make a mark on the top edge of the board. Do the same on the other side, then connect these marks with the bottom outside corners of the board with straight pencil lines. Cut away the wood outside these layout lines to form the basic shape of the end part.

The surest method of making a nice straight cut is to clamp a straight piece of scrap wood along the cut line to guide your saw. Cut on the waste side outside of the layout lines.

Next lay out and make the handholds in the ends. This 1⅛-inch-wide slot is centered 1⅝ inches from the top of each end. Measure down from the center mark placed along the top edge of the end and mark the center of the slot. From this center mark make another mark 2 inches to the right, then another 2 inches to the left. These marks are the points through which you should drill 1⅛-inch holes.

Use your brace and bit to make the holes. Place an end part on another board to protect your workbench from the point of the bit. To prevent the bit from tearing the wood as it exits the hole, turn the part over as soon as the point of the bit emerges from the back side of the wood and finish the holes from the opposite

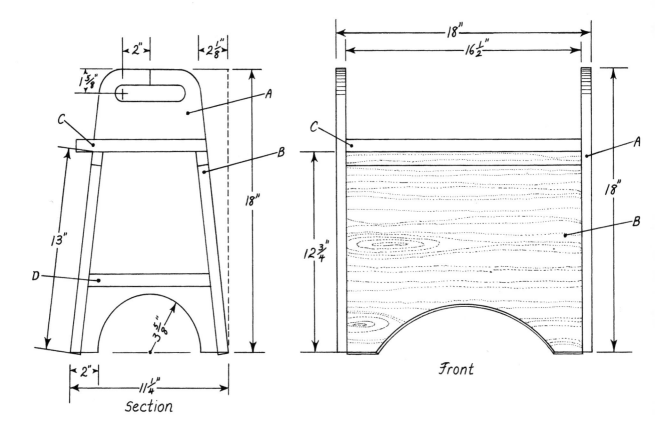

Section

Front

side. Then connect the holes with straight pencil lines and cut along the lines with a coping or keyhole saw to form the handhold slot.

When you have finished making the handhold slots in both parts, clamp them together. Then use your coping saw to round the top outer edge of these boards. Use a small bottle or other round object to lay out this curve. Place the bottle in the corner so it touches both edges and then trace around it to form an arc. A 2-inch radius works well here, but any arc pleasing to the eye will do. Cut both end parts at the same time.

Wrap sandpaper around a piece of scrap wood and sand away the saw marks from the arcs at the bottoms of the ends. With the parts clamped together you will be shaping both at the same time so they will be a matched pair. Also smooth the inside of the handhold slot. Use your plane to shave off any saw marks left on the edges. Plane both boards at the same time and you will find it easier to keep the edges even.

The front and back pieces are identical in size and shape. They are each made from two boards, upper and lower, since they are wider than wood carried at most lumberyards. The lower piece should be made from full-width one-by-twelve stock. The upper piece can be cut from any board at least 1¾ inches wide. Apply glue to the edges of these boards and clamp them together until the glue dries. With a sharp chisel, remove any glue that may have squeezed out of the joint.

The radius of the arc in the bottom panel of the front and back is 8 inches. Use a piece of string and a pencil to draw a circle with an 8-inch radius on a piece of cardboard. (Less than half the circle is needed.) To locate the arc on the wood make pencil marks on the bottom edge of the front 2 inches from each bottom corner. Place the cardboard circle on the wood and align its circumference with these marks, then trace the circle onto the wood. Use your

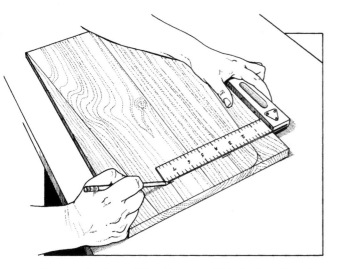

Lay out the shape of the side on an 18-inch piece of one-by-twelve stock. Then use a try square to lay out the center of the holes at each end of the handhold.

coping saw and cut on the waste side of the layout line. Mark and cut the corresponding panel for the back, then clamp the two parts together and sand the arc smooth.

Cut the top and bottom of the bench to size, sand the edges smooth, and then you are ready to assemble the bench. The ends are glued and nailed to the front and back with 6d finish nails that are located ⅜ inch from the edge of the end. Draw two layout lines on the ends ⅜ inch from the side edge to help you align the nails. Then predrive six evenly spaced nails along these layout lines. Apply glue to the ends of the front and back and nail the ends to them. Check alignment at the bottom and see that the side edges are flush. Drive the nails home but be careful not to mar the wood with your hammer. Install the front and back on one end first and then apply glue to the front and back and nail the other end in place. Set the bench upright and check that all legs sit on the ground.

Since the front and back pieces are angled, the bottoms of the legs of these pieces protrude slightly beyond the bottoms of the ends. Sand these small protrusions flush with the bottoms of the ends. You can also use a block plane to trim them flush.

In order for the bottom to fit between the slope of the front and back, the edges must be beveled slightly. Use your block plane and make a few passes on each long edge and then test the fit. Turn the bench upside down and drop the bottom into place to check its fit, beveled side down. The bottom should drop into the base of the bench far enough so it does not show below the arcs along the bottom edges of the front, back, and ends. Once you are satisfied with the fit, apply glue to the edges of the bottom, drop it in place, and secure it with 6d finish nails.

The top should fit loosely between the ends so it can open easily. Put it in position and plane one of its ends if the fit is too tight. The continuous hinge should be installed on the top first. At first use only a few of the screws; you can go back and install the rest after final alignment. Then put the top in place, open it, and align the hinge with the top edge of the back. Mark the location of the two outermost screws, remove the hinge, and drill a pilot hole through the marks. Replace the top and hinge and install the screws. Check that the top moves freely and then go back and install all of the screws provided with the hinge.

Use a chisel to remove any hardened glue that squeezed out of the joints and a nail set to set the nail heads below the surface of the wood. Then fill the holes with wood filler and when it has hardened give the bench a thorough sanding. Pay special attention to sanding all the curved edges so they are smooth.

Finish the bench with a light-colored wipe-on stain. But first wipe down the wood with wood conditioner to seal the end grain and assure an even finish on all of the wood surfaces. For added protection brush on a coat of polyurethane.

TOOLS

Hammer
Nail set
Measuring tape
Compass
Try square
Crosscut saw

Brace and bit with ½″
    and 1⅛″ bits
Hand drill with ⅛″ bit
Block plane
½″ wood chisel
Sanding block

PARTS LIST

	Part	Number	Size	Material
A	end	2	¾″ × 11¼″ × 18″	pine
B	front and back	2	¾″ × 13″ × 16½″	pine
C	top	1	¾″ × 9¼″ × 16½″	pine
D	bottom	1	¾″ × 8¾″ × 16½″	pine

MATERIALS LIST

Material	Amount	Size	Used For
1″ × 12″ pine	1	8 foot	end/front and back
1″ × 10″ pine	1	4 foot	top/bottom
¾″ continuous hinge	1	2 foot	
finish nails	1 box	6d	
carpenter's glue	1 small bottle		
120-grit sandpaper	2 sheets		

·Video/Audio Tape·
Storage Rack

As home electronic equipment invades our homes, most of us are faced with storing all the audiocassette tapes, VHS tapes, and CDs that go with them. A simple-to-build solution is this storage rack designed to keep everything in its place so that tapes and CDs are clearly visible and ready to use.

The construction combines pine end pieces connected by dowels with a sliding wooden divider that separates them.

How to Build It

The first step is to mark the length of the end parts on the one-by-ten board and then cut them to length. Next lay out the position of the dowels on the inside faces of the ends. The center of each dowel hole is located on the plan. The easiest way to locate these holes is to use your try square. Start laying out the holes from the back of the end parts, working toward the front. Look on the plan and note that the uppermost dowel (which supports the top of the audiocassette tape) is located 1⅛ inches in from the back edge and 12¼ inches up from the bottom back edge of the end.

To mark this spot, measure up the back edge 12¼ inches and then place the handle of the try square against the back edge with the top of the straightedge at the mark. Draw a line across the part. Then move the try square to the top edge and place the straightedge 1⅛ inches from the top back corner and draw a line that crosses the first line. This intersection marks the center of the first dowel. Follow this procedure to mark the center of the other five dowels on the end and then repeat the process on the other end part.

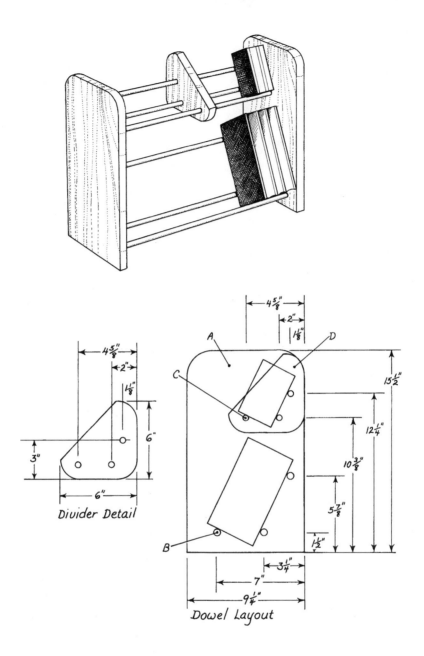

Divider Detail

Dowel Layout

Before you drill the ½-inch-deep, ½-inch-diameter holes for the dowels that support the VCR tapes and the $\frac{7}{16}$-inch-diameter holes for the dowels that hold the audio tapes, mark their centers. To do that use a nail set and punch a hole in the exact center of each layout line where they cross. This makes a small hole in the exact center of the dowel holes that helps prevent your bit from wandering off center. Place a piece of tape on the bit ½ inch from the tip so you can tell how deep the drill is going into the wood. Stop drilling when the tape touches the wood.

When you are finished making the dowel holes use your coping saw to round the upper corners of the ends. Our plan calls for a 2-inch radius at these corners. Use a compass to draw the arc from the top edge to the front edge or use any small round object like the base of a beverage glass or top of a jar to trace the arc. Place the round object in the corner so it touches both the upper and front edges and then trace around the shape to make the arc.

Using a coping saw, cut to the outside of the arc layout line and then clamp the parts together and smooth the edges with sandpaper. By working on them together, you'll sand both ends in the same shape.

The divider is made from a piece of scrap wood. Use the locations shown on the plan to lay out the position of the dowel with your try square. These holes are drilled completely through the wood so it can slide up and down the dowels. Mark the center of the holes with a nail set, then drill partially through one side until the point of the bit emerges from the wood on the other side. Then turn the part over and finish the hole from the back side to prevent tearing the wood as the bit comes out for a nice clean hole on both sides of the divider.

Test-fit a dowel in the holes. If the holes are too small, roll up a piece of sandpaper and run it through the holes to enlarge them slightly.

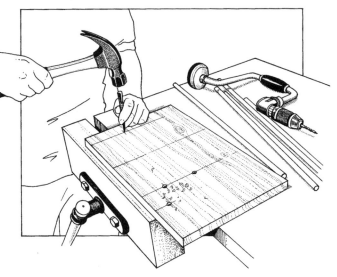

Lay out the dowel holes on the sides and mark their centers. Use a nail set to punch a hole in the exact center of the dowel holes so your drill starts on center.

For the divider to work it must be able to slide along the dowels easily.

Cut the dowels to length and then take a piece of sandpaper and smooth any rough edges off their ends; this makes it easier to insert the dowels into the ends.

When assembling the storage rack it does not matter which end you begin with. Place an end part on a flat surface with the dowel holes facing up. Apply a few drops of wood glue into each hole but do it sparingly. Be careful not to fill the hole. Then insert a dowel and push it into the hole. Use a twisting motion to force it as deeply into the hole as possible. Put a small piece of scrap wood on the end of the dowel to protect it and, with a hammer, tap the end gently to fully seat the dowel into its hole.

Slip the divider onto the upper dowels and check that it is oriented correctly. Then place the other end with the dowel holes up and put glue into the holes. It takes some coordination and adjustment because all the dowels must be inserted into their holes before you can begin to seat them securely. When all the dowels are worked into their mating holes, turn the rack over. Use the scrap wood to protect the upper end from the hammer head while you tap the end, driving the dowels into their holes as deeply as they go.

Place the rack upright on a flat surface and check that the ends are parallel to one another and perpendicular to the surface. If the rack is twisted and the ends don't touch the surface, turn them gently in the opposite direction. Make sure that the rack is square before the glue dries, because once the glue is dry, twisting the ends will break the glue joints between the dowels and ends, and the rack will not stay together.

After the glue has dried, chip away any glue residue that has squeezed out of the dowel joints. Then give the rack a careful sanding. Slide the divider up and down the dowels, and if it binds in some areas, spot-sand the dowel lightly where the divider is difficult to move.

TOOLS

Hammer	Crosscut saw
Measuring tape	Coping saw
Compass	Brace and bit with $\frac{1}{2}''$ bit
Try square	$\frac{1}{2}''$ wood chisel
Chisel	Sanding block

PARTS LIST

	Part	Number	Size	Material
A	end	2	$\frac{3}{4}'' \times 9\frac{1}{4}'' \times 15\frac{1}{2}''$	pine
B	divider	1	$\frac{3}{4}'' \times 6'' \times 6''$	pine
C	dowels	6	$\frac{1}{2}'' \times 19''$	hardwood
D	dowels	6	$\frac{7}{16}'' \times 19''$	hardwood

MATERIALS LIST

Material	Amount	Size	Used For
1″ × 10″ pine	1	3 foot	end/divider
½″ dowels	3	3 foot	videotape dowels
⁷⁄₁₆″ dowels	3	3 foot	audiotape dowels
carpenter's glue	1 small bottle		
120-grit sandpaper	2 sheets		

·Twig Side Table·

There's something very special about furniture made from tree branches. Maybe it's the fact that you get very involved right from the beginning walking through the woods gathering sturdy branches for the legs and smaller ones to act as braces.

Use a piece of cedar for the top and all-purpose screws to assemble the table. If you can't find wide cedar, join two narrower boards together with a few cleats of scrap wood nailed to the underside. Another good choice for the tabletop is a piece of weathered wood.

Use any species of wood that is available and convenient. When gathering branches to cut the twigs from, avoid those that have lain on the ground for a long time and those that show signs of rot or insect infestation.

You can make the table wider than the dimensions given if you want because it won't affect the dimensions of the legs; just increase

the length of the end trim pieces and the stretchers. If you make the table longer, just increase the length of the runner and the side trim pieces.

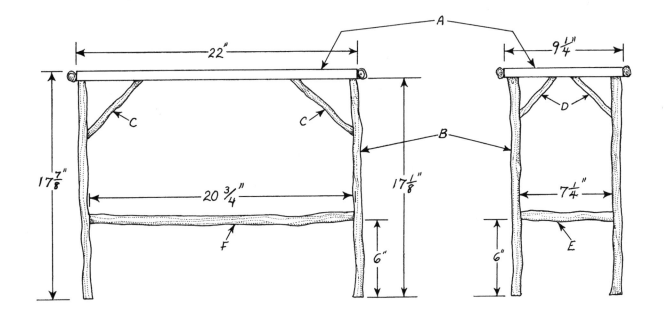

How to Build It

The dimensions provided are approximate and should be used as a guide. The only branches that should be carefully measured are the legs, since they must be the same length so the table stands straight and steady.

Cut the top to length and then drill a ⅛-inch hole in each corner for attaching the legs. Cut the legs to length from branches that are at least 1 inch in diameter. Then drill a ⅛-inch pilot hole in the center of the top of each leg. Attach the legs to the top with 1⅝-inch all-purpose screws driven through the top into the tops of the legs.

Cut four pieces of ½-inch-diameter twigs about 6 inches long to make the long braces.

Use a miter box to cut a 45-degree angle in each end. Check that the slants of the angles are the same on both ends. Then drill a ⅛-inch pilot hole through each end of these parts. You will find it is easier to drill these holes through the flat part of the 45-degree angle rather than through the rounded part of the twig. Put the long braces in position and use them as a template to drill matching pilot holes in the legs and underside of the top. Then install the braces with screws.

The short braces are made in the same way, only they should be cut about 4 inches long to fit the end of the table. Adjust their length so they don't intersect with the legs in the same spot as the long braces. This prevents the screw that attaches the parts to the legs from overlapping and weakening the leg.

Drill pilot holes in each end of the leg braces before installing them between the legs and the bottom of the tabletop.

runner and position it between the stretchers. Then drill through the stretchers and insert 2-inch screws into the holes and tighten them with a Phillips screwdriver.

The trim around the outside of the table is made from twigs that are about ½ inch in diameter, but just about any straight twigs will do. Hold the parts in place and then drill right through the twig into the edge of the top. Insert a 1⅝-inch screw into the hole and tighten it. Use at least four screws to install the side trim and three on the end trim.

Cut and fit the stretchers from 1-inch-diameter branches. Drill a pilot hole through each end of these parts. Also drill a pilot hole completely through the leg about 6 inches from the bottom. Then put the stretchers in position and drive the 2-inch screws through the legs into the ends of the leg ties.

Next measure the distance between the stretchers and cut a piece of 1-inch-diameter branch to this dimension. This piece will be your runner. Drill pilot holes in each end of the

Insert 2-inch screws into the holes and tighten them with a Phillips screwdriver.

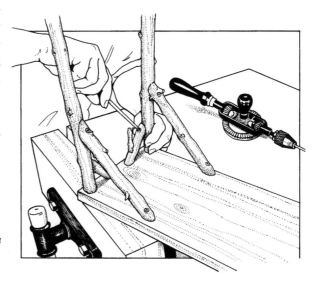

105

TOOLS

Measuring tape
Try square
Saw
Hand drill and bits

PARTS LIST

Part		Number	Size	Material
A	top	1	¾″ × 9¼″ × 22″	cedar
B	leg	4	1″ dia., 17″ long	branch
C	long brace	4	½″ dia., 6″ long	branch
D	short brace	4	½″ dia., 4″ long	branch
E	stretcher	2	1″ dia., 7¼″ long	branch
F	runner	1	1″ dia., 20¾″ long	branch
G	side trim	2	1″ dia., 23″ long	branch
H	end trim	2	1″ dia., 9¼″ long	branch

MATERIALS LIST

Material	Amount	Size	Used For
1″ × 10″ cedar board	1	2 foot	top
tree branch	20 feet	1″ dia.	legs/stretcher/runner
tree branch	4 feet	½″ dia.	long/short leg brace
all-purpose screws	1 box	1⅝″	

· Footstool ·

This footstool does a lot more than provide a nice resting place for weary feet. Use it for reaching up to a top shelf or to change light-bulbs in a ceiling fixture. Use it as pint-size furniture for visiting youngsters. It's just the right size for a child to sit on or to use as a desk for a coloring book while kneeling on the floor.

The footstool can be made of oak or pine boards, which are both durable material and will withstand years of use and abuse. There are five parts: two sides, two aprons, and one top.

How to Build It

The legs require the most work, so begin with them. Each leg has a 3-inch-radius arc in its bottom and notches at the tops of its sides. It is easier to make these arcs by cutting a circle first. Then the individual legs can be cut apart.

Cut a piece of one-by-ten lumber 24 inches long. Use a try square to draw a straight pencil line across the board 12 inches from either end. Then lay out a circle with a 3-inch radius in the center of the board on this line. Use your brace and bit to drill a $\frac{1}{2}$-inch hole inside the circle but close to its edge. With a coping saw cut along the circular layout line and remove the circle. Cut this piece in half along the center line to form the two legs, each 12 inches long.

Next use your try square to lay out the position of the notches in the sides of each leg. These notches are $\frac{1}{2}$ inch deep and $3\frac{1}{2}$ inches long. Use a backsaw to cut inside the layout lines. Remove the waste piece and then clean up the notch with your chisel so that the wood is smooth. Square up the notch with the layout lines.

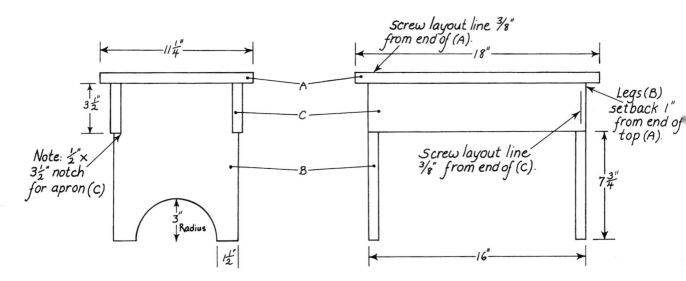

When the notches are cut in both legs, clamp them together and smooth the arc at the bottom with sandpaper. As you sand away the saw marks you'll see that the arcs are the same shape since you are working on both at the same time.

The aprons are the pieces of wood that hold the legs together. Cut these parts from the one-by-four stock. When making these cuts be sure to leave the layout lines, which means cutting on the waste side of the line. After assembly the ends of the aprons can be sanded perfectly smooth and flush with faces of the legs.

These parts are held firmly to the legs with

glue and screws that are covered with wood plugs. Make pilot holes for the screws and plugs located ⅜ inch from the end of the apron. Use your try square to make a straight line across the board ⅜ inch from its end. Then use your brace and bit to drill ⅜-inch holes 1 inch from each edge centered on the line. Drill carefully and make these holes only ⅜ inch deep to hold the plugs. Drill ⅛-inch holes through the center of the larger holes for the screws.

Cut the top to size and ease all its edges with your block plane. Be careful cutting across the end grain with the plane. Work the plane toward the center of the board when planing the end grain to prevent tearing out a piece of wood at the corner.

At this stage you are ready to test-fit the parts. Put the sides and aprons together and if necessary adjust the notches so the aprons fit tightly and are flush with the tops of the legs. While you are holding the aprons in place, use them as a template and make a pencil mark through each screw hole to locate the position of these screws on the sides of the legs. Then remove the apron and drill a ⅛-inch pilot hole through each mark.

Assemble the legs and aprons with glue and screws. To help keep things square, place the aprons on a flat surface and install the legs upside down. Apply glue to the sides of the legs in the notch area. Then screw the aprons to the legs with 1¼-inch all-purpose screws. Check that the legs are perpendicular to the aprons with a try square. Drive one screw home and check alignment again; then install the other one. After you have the legs and aprons together set the assembly aside on a flat surface to allow the glue to dry.

In the side of each leg, cut the notches that receive the sides with a backsaw or other fine-toothed saw.

The top is held to the base assembly with glue and screws. These screws are located 1⅛ inches from the edge and 1⅜ inches from the ends. Lay out four evenly spaced screws along the ends and sides. To do this, draw pencil layout lines 1⅛ inches from the edge and 1⅜ inches from the ends and mark the screw locations along the lines. Drill a shallow ⅜-inch hole through each mark to accommodate the wood plugs and then drill a ⅛-inch pilot hole through the centers of the holes for the screws.

Place the top on the leg assembly so it has a 1-inch overhang on the ends and ¾ inch on the sides. Then mark the locations of the screws on the legs and apron with a pencil through the holes in the top. Remove the top and drill ⅛-inch pilot holes through these layout marks.

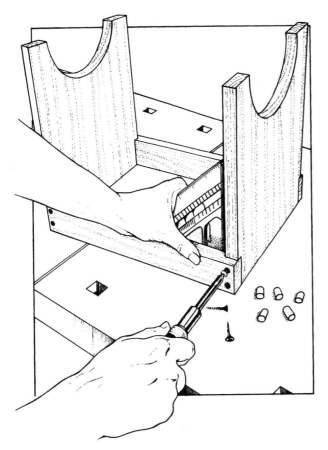

Carefully apply glue to the tops of the legs and aprons and position the top on this assembly. Then drive the screws home (into the wood). After the top is secured, put a dab of glue on the ends of the wood plugs and fill all the screw holes with the plugs.

When the glue has set, use a sharp chisel to cut the plugs off about ⅛ inch from the surface. Chip away any dried glue that might have squeezed out of a joint with your chisel. Then grind the plugs flush with the surface of the wood using sandpaper wrapped around a block of wood. Give all the parts of the bench a careful sanding, especially the areas under any chipped-off glue marks.

To finish the footstool, begin with a wipe-on wood conditioner to seal the cut-out arcs in the legs and the end grain of the plugs. You can add color with a stain followed by a topcoat of polyurethane for protection or use polyurethane only to show the natural light color of the pine.

Place the legs and sides on a flat surface while assembling to assure that the unit is square. Fill the screw head holes with wood plugs.

TOOLS

Hammer
Measuring tape
Compass
Try square
Crosscut saw

Brace and bit with ½″
    and ⅜″ bits
Hand drill with ⅛″ bit
½″ wood chisel
Sanding block

PARTS LIST

Part		Number	Size	Material
A	top	1	¾″ × 11¼″ × 18″	oak or pine
B	leg	2	¾″ × 9¼″ × 11¼″	oak or pine
C	apron	2	¾″ × 3½″ × 16″	oak or pine

MATERIALS LIST

Material	Amount	Size	Used For
1″ × 12″ oak or pine	1	2 feet	top
1″ × 10″ oak or pine	1	2 feet	leg
1″ × 4″ oak or pine	1	4 feet	apron
all-purpose screws	16	#8 1¼″	
oak or pine wood plugs	2 doz.	⅜″	
carpenter's glue	1 small bottle		
120-grit sandpaper	4 sheets		

·Airplane Whirligig·

It's not easy to decide which is more fun: build-ing a whirligig or watching it catch the wind and perform. We designed this airplane whirli-gig with a propeller that harnesses the power of the wind to make it rotate. Mount it on a mail-box stand or fence post, and it's sure to delight passersby.

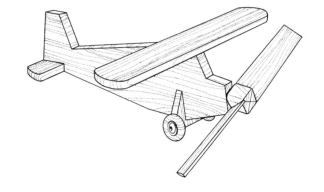

How to Build It

Since this whirligig does not have many mechanical parts it is very easy to build—per-fect for the first-time whirligig builder. The body of the plane is cut from one-by-six com-mon lumber, and the wings, tail, and landing gear are cut from ½-inch-thick stock. If you have trouble locating ½-inch-thick wood, look in the molding section of your lumberyard, because you can substitute wide lattice or mul-lion stock for this wood. If you can't find ½-inch board there is no reason why the wing, tail, and landing gear can't be made from the same lumber as the body. They will be a trifle thick-looking and slightly out of scale with the body, but then this is a whirligig and not a scale model.

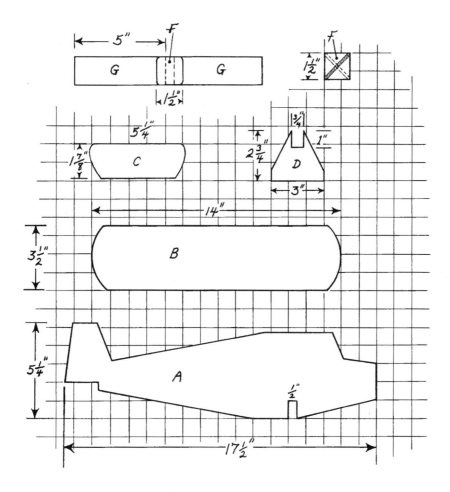

Use the grid pattern provided to lay out the shape of the plane's body on the one-by-six stock. Then use your coping saw to cut the body to shape. Cut the wings and tail to rough size and then transfer the shape of the wing tip from the grid pattern provided to the ends of the wood. Cut the wing tips to shape with your coping saw.

The landing gear is cut from a wood block 2½ inches high and 2¾ inches wide. Lay out its shape on the wood. Cut the ¾-inch-wide, 1-inch-deep notch in the center of the top first, then cut the shoulders.

The propeller is not hard to make because it does not have to be precisely balanced. Make the prop hub by gluing two 1½-inch-square blocks, cut from the ¾-inch stock, together so you come up with a cube measuring 1½ inches on each side. While the glue is drying, cut the prop blades to size and give them a good sanding to round any rough edges. Sand them as a pair so they stay the same shape.

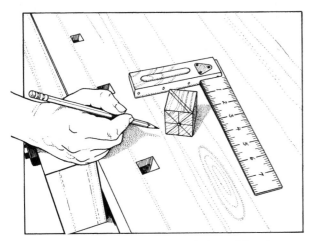

Mark the hub on two opposite sides with diagonal lines from corner to corner. When cut out, these slots will accommodate the two propeller blades.

After the glue has dried, sand the sides of the block smooth to remove any traces of glue and any saw marks. Lay out the position of the prop blades by drawing a diagonal line from corner to corner. On the side opposite the one you just drew the line on, draw another line from corner to corner but make this line connect the opposite set of opposing corners. You must do this so the blade will have a pitch opposite the one on the other side of the hub. Use the blade as a template and mark its location on the hub. Place the blade on the side of the layout toward the center of the hub, then draw a pencil line down the other side of the blade to mark its thickness on the hub. Do the same for the other blade on the opposite side of the hub.

Use a backsaw or coping saw to cut the ½-inch-deep notches for the blades in the prop hub. Keep your saw cuts inside the layout lines;

you can go back and make the slot wider with a piece of sandpaper. Test-fit the blades into the hub and adjust the slots for a snug fit. Then round the corners of the hub with sandpaper. Apply glue to the slots and the ends for the blades and insert them into the hub. Place the hub facedown on a flat surface and make sure the blades are straight and that both make contact with the flat surface.

Drill a ⅛-inch hole through the center of the hub for the #6 RH mounting screw. The propeller will turn on the mounting screw and a couple of washers between the prop hub and the plane body. The prop does turn very fast in a good breeze, so eventually this hole will begin to enlarge from wear. A short piece of ¼-inch-diameter copper tubing inserted into the hub acts as a bearing to prevent this.

Assembly of the plane is straightforward. Use 3d finish nails and glue to attach the wings to the top of the body. Attach the tail to the underside of the body with the same glue and nails. Glue the landing gear to the body and hold it in place until the glue dries with a couple of nails driven through the body at an angle into the landing gear. Then install ready-made 1½-inch wheels, available at a hobby store or through mail order (see page 2 for mail-order information) with the #5 RH screws. Drill ⅛-inch pilot holes in the landing gear to prevent splitting the wood.

Painting the plane is almost as much fun as making it. Any paint that can be used outdoors will be fine for this project. Give your plane a good sanding and a coat of exterior oil primer before you apply the final coat and you will have a paint job that will hold up.

The whirligig is mounted on a post so it can pivot into the wind. Having a friction-reducing bearing in this joint helps allow the plane to turn into the wind even in light air. Use a ¼-inch ball bearing for this purpose. Drill a 2-inch-deep, ¼-inch-diameter hole in the bottom of the plane's body just behind the landing gear. Then drop the ball bearing into the hole and hold it in place with a 2-inch length of copper tubing driven into the hole.

Make the pivot out of a 16d nail. Just cut the head off the nail and install it on the end of your mounting post. Drill a ⅛-inch hole for the nail and tap it into the end of the post. Then slip the plane on the nail and it will pivot nicely into the wind.

TOOLS

Hammer
Measuring tape
Try square
Coping saw
Backsaw
Hand drill and bits
Sanding block

PARTS LIST

	Part	Number	Size	Material
A	body	1	¾″ × 5¼″ × 17⅝″	pine
B	wing	1	½″ × 3½″ × 14″	pine
C	tail	1	½″ × ⅞″ × 5¼″	pine
D	landing gear	1	½″ × 2½″ × 2¾″	pine
E	wheels	2	1½″ dia.	hardwood
F	prop hub	2	¾″ × 1½″ × 1½″	pine
G	prop blade	2	¼″ × 2″ × 5″	pine

MATERIALS LIST

Material	Amount	Size	Used For
1″ × 6″ pine	1	2 foot	body/prop hub
½″ pine	1	2 foot	wing/tail/landing gear
1¼″ lattice	1	2 foot	prop blade
hardwood wheels	2	1½″ dia.	
#5 RH brass wood screw and washers	1	3″	
#5 RH brass wood screw and washers	2	1″	
¼″ dia. copper tubing	1	6″	
steel ball bearing	1	¼″ dia.	
carpenter's glue	1 small bottle		
finish nails	1 box	3d	
120-grit sandpaper	2 sheets		

· Birdhouse ·

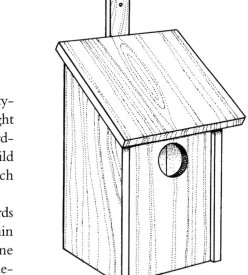

Bluebirds and other cavity-nesting birds will feel right at home in our cedar birdhouse. It is easy to build using ⅜-inch cedar, which also makes it lightweight.

At some lumberyards where they don't stock thin wood they offer to plane wood to the thickness desired and charge a small fee for the service. For this birdhouse, have a 4-foot-long piece of one-by-eight cedar planed down to be ⅜ inch thick.

How to Build It

Although the parts for this project are cut from a large board, the wood is thin and easy to cut.

To save some time, cut off an 18-inch section of the one-by-eight board to form two pieces for the sides. Then rip that piece to a 5-inch width and set it aside. Cut off a 7-inch piece from the remaining length to make the roof.

Rip (cut lengthwise) the remaining 4½-foot length of wood to 4¼ inches wide to make the front, bottom, and back.

To cut the sides, measure 9 inches up from the bottom corner of the 18-inch piece and make a mark. On the opposite edge measure up 7 inches from the bottom front edge and make a mark. Then connect these points on the back edge with those on the front with a pencil line. Cut along this layout line and keep your saw

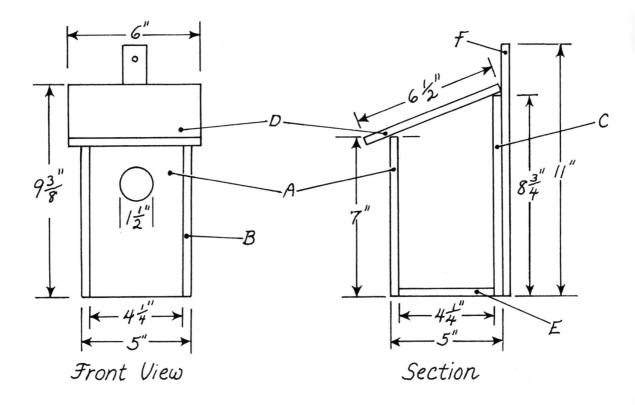

Front View

Section

on the line because you are cutting both parts at once. Then clamp the parts together and remove saw marks from the top edges by sanding. Also trim them at the bottom if they are not exactly the same length. To get nice square edges use the shooting board and plane to dress up all cuts (see pages 134–37 for instructions for making a shooting board).

Cut the front, bottom, and back from the 4¼-inch-wide board. Take care to make the cuts as square as possible. You will get a more accurate cut if you lay out and then saw off each part sequentially. Start at one end and measure the length of the part. Don't mark lay-

out lines for all three parts on the board and then cut them to length, because the parts will not be accurate.

Use your try square to draw a straight layout line across the board. Then cut the part, keeping outside this line. Repeat this process for the other two parts. Make the roof from the remaining piece of wood and cut it so the wood grain runs down the slope parallel to the 6-inch edge. Rip the 1⅛-inch-wide hanger part from the remaining scrap wood.

Assembly is easy, but be careful nailing close to the ends of the parts because the cedar may split. Make pilot holes to prevent the wood

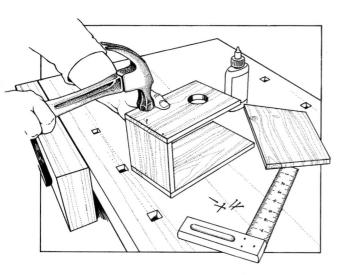

First nail the back of the birdhouse to the bottom, then nail the front to the bottom to form a U-shaped assembly. Nail the side to the back, then to the front.

from splitting and use small brads for nailing. Cut off the head of a brad and place the shaft of the brad into your drill and use it as a bit to drill the pilot holes.

Lay out the location of the entrance hole on the front. The center of the 1½-inch hole is located 2 inches down from the top. Mark its location and then use a nail set to make a small starter hole through the point. Bore the hole with a brace and 1½-inch bit.

Nail the hanger strip to the back of the unit. Make sure you drive a brad into the edge of the bottom and again be careful not to split the wood. Then drive a few more brads through the hanger into the back. The brads will come

out of the back and should be bent over to lock them in place and prevent the birds from being injured by them.

You can put the house parts together in just about any sequence. Nailing the front and back to the bottom first and then installing the sides is an easy method. First nail the front to the bottom with four evenly spaced 1-inch wire brads. Then nail the back to the bottom with the same number of brads. Place this U-shaped assembly on its side and then place a side part on it. Align the back flush with the back edge of the side and the bottom flush with the bottom edge of the side. Nail the side to the back first, then to the bottom. Then carefully align the front so it is parallel with the front edge of the side; there should be a ¼-inch setback between the side and the front. Hold the front in position while you drive the brads through the side and then flip the unit over and nail on the other side.

The roof is nailed to the top edges of the sides. To help locate the position of the brads, put the top in place and then run a pencil point along each side so it makes a line on the underside of the top. Turn the top over and use these lines as a guide when placing the nails. The nails go just inside this line because they are driven into the center of the top edge of the sides.

Your birdhouse is ready for its first tenant. Cedar will hold up well without any special finishes. We recommend a coat of a clear water sealer to keep it looking good longer.

TOOLS

Hammer
Try square
Tape measure
Saw
Brace and 1½″ bit

PARTS LIST

	Part	Number	Size	Material
A	front	1	⅜″ × 4¼″ × 7″	cedar
B	side	2	⅜″ × 5″ × 9″	cedar
C	back	1	⅜″ × 4¼″ × 8¾″	cedar
D	roof	1	⅜″ × 6″ × 6½″	cedar
E	bottom	1	⅜″ × 4¼″ × 4¼″	cedar
F	hanger	1	⅜″ × 1⅛″ × 11″	cedar

MATERIALS LIST

Material	Amount	Size	Used For
1″ × 8″ cedar board	1	6 foot	all parts
wire brads	1 box	1″	
carpenter's glue	1 small bottle		
120-grit sandpaper	1 sheet		

·Kids' Wagon·

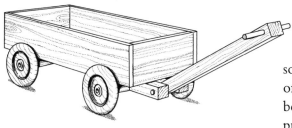

Here's a pull toy any child will enjoy. Fill it up with wooden building blocks or a cuddly koala bear, and it's sure to be a favorite toy for little ones who like to bring along their stash of treasures wherever they go.

How to Build It

To make this wagon easy to build we designed its construction around readily available molding and lattice stock. You can find both lattice

and baluster stock at a lumberyard or home center. The wagon does not require any part to be longer than 12 inches, so you can purchase short leftovers, which are often sold after the long pieces of molding have been cut to custom lengths. The wheels can be purchased at a hobby store or through mail-order sources (see page 2) and come with matching axle pins.

The bottom of the wagon can be made out of just about any type of wood, such as a short section of one-by-six lumber or a scrap of ¾-inch plywood.

Cut all the parts to length and use your miter box so the ends of all parts are nice and square. The sides and ends are cut from lattice. The axle supports, handle, and the three parts that make up the handle support are cut from ¾-inch-square baluster stock.

Assembly is quick because only a few brads

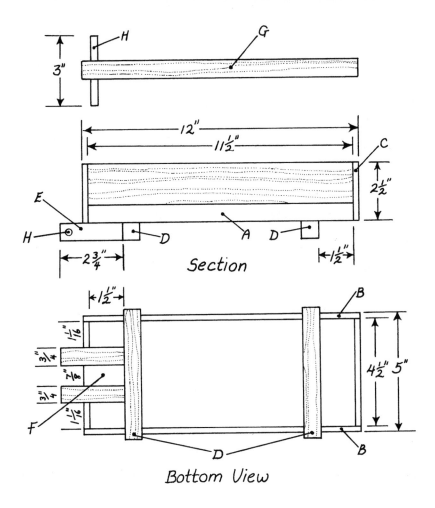

Section

Bottom View

are needed. Glue holds the wagon together. Start with the axle supports and drill a ⅜-inch hole in the center of each end to take the wheel axle pins. Use a pencil to draw a straight line from corner to corner so these lines cross in the center of the piece. Mark this point by driving your nail set into the end of the axle support through the intersection of the layout lines. The small hole made by the point of the nail set gives your drill a pilot hole in the center so it won't wander off center as you drill. Drill the ⅜-inch hole about 1-inch deep and then repeat the process on the other three ends of the axle support.

The axle supports are glued and nailed to the bottom piece 1½ inches from each end of the wagon. Apply glue to the axle supports and then position them so that there is a ¼-inch overlap on each side of the bottom. Hold them in place with a few 1¼-inch wire brads.

Next install the hand support assembly. This unit is composed of a handle spacer sandwiched between the two handle yokes. This assembly is located flush against the axle support and 1⅛

Use wood glue and 1 ¼-inch wire brads to fasten the axles and the parts that make up the handle support to the bottom.

the sides to the edge of the bottom and the edge of the end parts. You need three or four brads to hold the sides in place, but be careful when you drive a brad through the edge of the side; you're dealing with thin wood and it can split. To prevent this, drill a ¹⁄₁₆-inch pilot hole for these brads. If you don't have a drill bit this small you can cut the head off a brad and place it in your drill to act as a drill bit to make these holes.

After the glue has dried remove any excess with a sharp chisel and then give all the surfaces of the wagon a light sanding. For a natural-looking wagon use an easy-to-apply wipe-on oil finish. If you used scraps of mismatched lumber to build this project you may be better off painting the wagon so it is a uniform color.

You can finish the handle in the same way or leave it natural.

When the finish has hardened, add the wheels and axle pins. To install them put a drop of glue in the holes you drilled in the ends of the axle supports, put the wheel on the axle pin, and push the pin into the hole. Don't push the pin in too far because the wheels need a little play to turn freely.

To install the handle, cut a 2¼-inch piece of ⅜-inch dowel to form the handle pin and push it into the holes you drilled in the handle supports. Place the handle between the handle supports and push the pin all the way in. It should be a tight fit, so if the dowel is loose, back it out a bit and apply a drop of glue to the hole and push the pin back into position. Drill a ⅜-inch hole in the other end of the handle for a 3-inch section of dowel that forms an easy-grip handle. Glue the dowel in place.

inches from either side of the bottom. Glue and nail these parts in place with 1¼-inch brads.

You have to drill a ⅜-inch-diameter hole through the handle supports and handle to accept the handle pin that holds the pieces together. The easiest way to locate this point is to draw a straight line with a try square across the handle support ¾ inch from the end of the part. Then connect the two outside corners of the part with the opposite ends of the line. These lines will intersect in the center of the part. Then make a pilot hole with a nail set through the intersection. Place the handle in the yoke assembly and drill a ⅜-inch hole at the mark and completely through the yoke assembly and handle.

Cut the sides and ends to length and then nail them in place beginning with the ends. Make sure that the ends are flush with the sides and lower edge of the bottom. Glue and nail

TOOLS

Measuring tape   Crosscut saw
Try square   Brace and ⅜″ bit
Hammer   Hand drill and bits
Nail set

PARTS LIST

	Part	Number	Size	Material
A	bottom	1	¾″ × 4½″ × 11½″	pine
B	side	2	¼″ × 2½″ × 12″	pine lattice
C	end	2	¼″ × 2½″ × 4½″	pine lattice
D	axle support	2	¾″ × ¾″ × 5½″	pine
E	handle yoke	2	¾″ × ¾″ × 2¾″	pine
F	handle spacer	1	¾″ × ¾″ × 1¾″	pine
G	handle	1	¾″ × ¾″ × 12″	pine
H	handle pin	1	⅜″ dia. × 3″	dowel
I	handle pivot	1	⅜″ dia. × 2½″	dowel

MATERIALS LIST

Material	Amount	Size	Used For
2½″ lattice	1	3 foot	sides/ends
1″ × 6″ pine	1	1 foot	bottom
¾″ baluster stock	1	3 foot	handle parts/axle support
⅜″ dia. dowel	1	3 foot	handle pin/pivot
wood wheels	4	2¾″	wheels (Klockit #35385)
wood axles	4	⅜″	wheels (Klockit #35926)
wire brads	1 box	1¼″	
carpenter's glue	1 small bottle		
120-grit sandpaper	2 sheets		

•Tile Flower Tray•

Here's a stylish way to dress up an arrangement of flowerpots while providing a convenient tray to catch drips and spills when watering the plants. The tile flower tray comes in handy on windowsills or on a shelf or wherever you display pots of fresh plants.

We designed the tray for 4-inch tiles and used 1-inch pine lattice as edging around the sides of the tiles, allowing room for adhesive caulk in between them.

If you choose to use other size tiles, check the fit of tiles and caulk before you cut the base, in case you have to make an adjustment. To ensure an adequate fit, place tiles together as they will appear on the tray and measure the overall dimensions. If the length and width of your tile is the same or smaller than the dimensions given in the Parts List for the base, everything will fit. Otherwise add ¼ inch to the length and width of your tiles and cut the base

to this size. The ends will then be the exact width of the base and the sides are ½ inch longer than the length of the base.

How to Build It

Building this project takes very little time. Begin by cutting the base to size from a piece of scrap plywood. Plywood can be cut with either a ripsaw or a crosscut saw since its grain is different in each layer of laminate. Then cut the end and side pieces to length.

Nail and glue the ends to the base with 1-inch wire brads and carpenter's glue. Apply glue to the edges of the base and check that the ends of the end parts are flush with the sides of the base. Then nail them together.

Glue and nail the sides in place in exactly

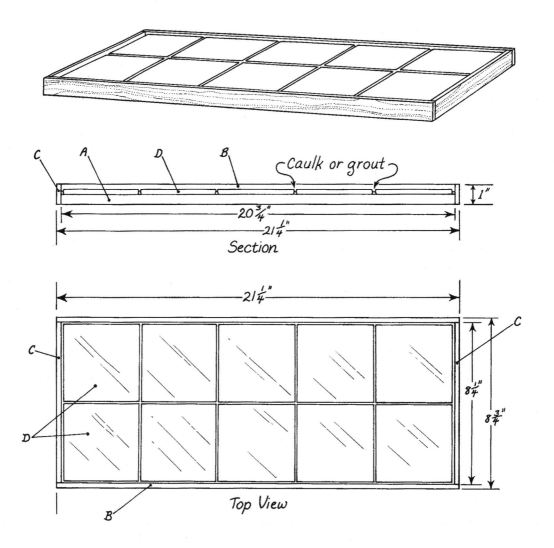

Section

Caulk or grout

Top View

the same way. If they overlap the ends slightly don't worry, because you can trim them flush after the glue has dried. When the glue is dry, sand the ends of the sides flush with the ends.

Use a nail set to drive the heads of the brads below the wood surface and then fill the holes with wood filler. Then sand the sides flush with the ends and ease all the sharp corners slightly with a sanding block.

It is easier to stain or paint the tray base before you apply the tiles. If you plan to use the tray outside, give it a coat of exterior finish or paint.

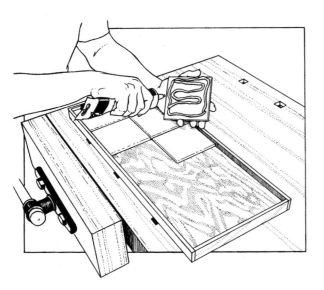

Install the 4-inch-square tiles with adhesive caulk or use tile mastic if you have some left over from another project. Apply a liberal amount of caulk from the tube, spreading it in an S pattern. Push the tile into place and wiggle it back and forth to spread the caulk between the tile and the plywood. When all the tiles are in place, go back and apply caulk to the joints between the tiles and between the tiles and the wood frame. Use a wet finger to smooth the caulk lines. With a wet rag remove any excess caulk from the faces of the tiles.

Apply adhesive caulk or tile mastic to the back of the tiles to secure them to the base of the tray.

TOOLS

Hammer
Nail set
Measuring tape
Crosscut saw
Sanding block

PARTS LIST

	Part	Number	Size	Material
A	base	1	½″ × 8¼″ × 20¾″	plywood
B	side	2	¼″ × 1″ × 21¼″	pine lattice
C	end	2	¼″ × 1″ × 8¼″	pine lattice
D	tiles	10	¼″ × 4″ × 4″	ceramic tiles

MATERIALS LIST

Material	Amount	Size	Used For
½″ plywood	1	scrap	base
1″ lattice	1	6 foot	sides/ends
ceramic tiles	10	4″	tray top
wire brads	1 box	1″	
carpenter's glue	1 small bottle		
adhesive caulk	1 tube		
120-grit sandpaper	2 sheets		

•Toolbox with Strap•

Having the right tool on hand for a job helps make a repair or maintenance project run smoothly, so we designed a tool tote to hold the various hand tools you'll assemble in your collection. The box is divided into two compartments: a narrow area for small items so they are clearly visible and not concealed by heavier tools, and a larger space for bulkier tools. You can add a detachable shoulder strap that makes the box easier to carry from one job to another.

How to Build It

For the most part, this project is constructed of dimensional wood. The divider and ends are cut from common one-by-twelve lumber. Although the layout of the ends is easy, we've provided a pattern. First cut the one-by-twelve stock into two 8-inch-by-9¼-inch pieces. Then transfer the outline of the ends to these pieces and cut them to size.

The divider is cut from a full-size piece of one-by-twelve stock. Cut the board to length (28½ inches) and mark its center, which is 14¼ inches from either end. The center of the opening for the handhold is located 1 inch from the top edge of the board and aligned with the mark. The center of the 1⅛-inch holes that make up the ends of the handhold are located 2⅜ inches from the center line and 1⅞ inches down from the upper edge. Use a try square to lay out these points and then bore a 1⅛-inch hole through them with your brace

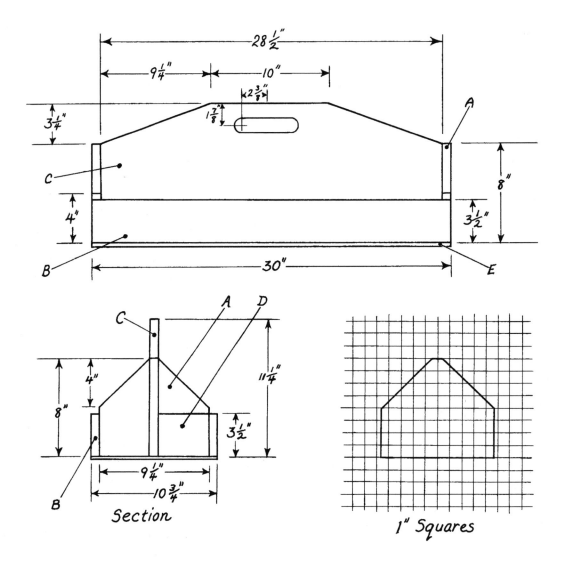

Section

1" Squares

and bit. To create a nice, cleanly cut hole, drill only halfway through the board and then turn it over and complete the hole from the opposite side. Connect the holes with straight lines and then use a coping saw to cut along the lines to form the handhold.

Use the dimensions shown to lay out and then cut the angled edges of the top of the divider using a fine ten- or twelve-point cross-cut saw. Then plane these edges smooth to remove any saw marks. The sides and partitions are cut from one-by-four stock. The bottom is cut from a quarter sheet of ¼-inch-thick plywood.

Assembly of the toolbox is straightforward. Begin by nailing the partitions to the divider with 4d finish nails. The location of these partitions is not critical; place them where you think they will be most useful. You can make a large compartment for long 16d nails and small compartments for shorter nails—it's up to you. Drive the nails through the divider into the edge of the partition. To make this easier, offset the compartments slightly on opposite sides of the divider.

Next glue and nail the ends to the divider. Use 6d finish nails and carpenter's glue to strengthen the joint. To help position the nails, draw a pencil line down the center of the end and drive four evenly spaced 6d nails into the end along this line. Check that the bottom edges of these parts are flush. Then apply glue to the edge of the divider and nail the end in place.

Complete the toolbox frame by gluing and nailing the sides to the ends. Use 6d finish nails and place them ⅜ inch from the end of the side. Drill pilot holes for the nails to prevent the wood from splitting. If you don't have a ¹⁄₁₆-inch drill bit, cut the head off a nail and use it in your drill as a bit to make the holes. Check that the bottom edges of the sides, partitions, and ends are all flush so they make contact with the bottom.

Recheck the final dimensions of the bottom of the toolbox. Then cut the bottom to these dimensions. Cut on the outside of your layout lines. It is better that the bottom be slightly oversized than undersized since you can plane away any overhang to make it flush with the sides.

Glue and nail the bottom in place with 1½-inch roofing nails. Apply glue to the edges of

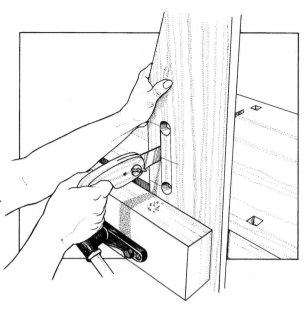

Drill holes at the end of the handhold, then use a keyhole or coping saw to cut along the straight layout line you drew between the edges of these holes.

the divider and ends but not to the partitions. This lets you remove the partitions and reposition them at a later time if you find they'd work better elsewhere. Check that the bottom is cut square and then nail it to the frame. You may have to push the frame into alignment with the bottom for a good fit.

After the glue has dried, round all edges with a sanding block. Wrap sandpaper around a dowel or pencil to sand the inside of the handhold. Your toolbox is ready to go, but it can get heavy when you fill it up so here's an idea for a shoulder strap. Buy a web nylon strap with two end clips called a lawn trimmer strap. It's an accessory for carrying a lawn trimmer on your shoulder that is sold in the garden section of home centers. It attaches to eye bolts you can easily screw into opposite ends of the box.

TOOLS

Measuring tape   Crosscut saw
Try square   Coping or keyhole saw
Hammer   Brace and 1⅛″ bit
Nail set   Hand drill and bits
Screwdriver

PARTS LIST

Part		Number	Size	Material
A	end	2	¾″ × 8″ × 9¼″	pine
B	side	2	¾″ × 3½″ × 30″	pine
C	divider	1	¾″ × 11¼″ × 28½″	pine
D	partition	4	¾″ × 3½″ × 4½″	pine
E	bottom	1	¼″ × 10¾″ × 30″	plywood

MATERIALS LIST

Material	Amount	Size	Used For
1″ × 4″ pine	1	6 foot	side/partitions
1″ × 12″ pine	1	6 foot	divider/end
¼″ plywood	1	¼ sheet	bottom
finish nails	1 box	4d	
finish nails	1 box	6d	
1¼″ roofing nails	1 box		
carpenter's glue	1 small bottle		
lawn trimmer strap	1		
eye bolts	2		
120-grit sandpaper	2 sheets		

· Woodworking Jigs ·

These workshop aids will help you make better use of your hand tools. The bench hook is designed to be placed on a workbench to protect its surface from scarring or damage. The two shooting boards are frames that hold a board while its edge is being planed either on top of a workbench or in a miter box. As you work with hand tools, no doubt you'll come up with your own custom workbench helpers.

How to Build a Bench Hook

The bench hook isn't really a hook at all. It helps when you're cutting a piece of wood by holding it secure and square to the saw. The base of the bench hook also protects your workbench from the saw. The bench hook has only

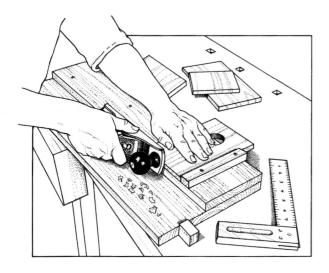

Use the shooting board to square up the end of a board. Place it against the stop, then lay your plane on its side on the base and plane the end of the part.

three parts—a base and two fences—which can be cut from just about any type of wood.

Cut the base to length and then rip the fences to size. Use your bench plane to cut a ¼-inch chamfer on an edge of one of the fences. A chamfer is a beveled edge formed at a right-angle corner that provides a small recess in which sawdust can collect instead of getting between your work and the fence.

It is best to install the fences without nails or screws so you can cut through the fence with your saw and not have to worry about dulling the saw blade should it strike a nail or screw. Apply glue to the face of the fence that has the chamfered edge. Then place the fence on the base and carefully align it flush with the back edge of the base. Clamp it in place and recheck to see that it has not moved. It is important that the fence is installed parallel to the edge of the base and flush with its back edge. When the glue has set up on the first fence, glue the other one to the underside of the base along the opposite edge.

To use the bench hook, place it on the workbench and slide it inward until the lower fence is against the edge of the bench. Then place your work on the hook and push it tight against the top fence. This setup allows you to hold your work squarely on the bench without having to clamp it down.

Before you use the bench hook, make a cut through the top fence about 2 inches from its end. Use a try square to align the saw and try to make the cut perpendicular to the base. Then you can use this groove, or kerf, as a reference when cutting boards on the bench hook. When the kerf gets worn, make another one. When cutting the end of a board it is helpful to have this slot to put your saw in to start the cut.

The bench hook is also useful for holding work that has to be drilled. Use it to hold any board that you may drill through to prevent damage to the face of your workbench. When the bench hook gets full of holes and the fences are all cut up, make a new one.

How to Build a Shooting Board

Since most of the projects in this book are small, a 2-foot-long shooting board will serve you well. They are easy to make, so if you have long boards to true up you can also make a longer version.

Cut the base and ramp to length. The underside of the ramp has a ¼-inch chamfer cut into it just like the bench hook. Use your bench plane to cut this chamfer and then glue and screw the ramp to the base using 1¼-inch #6 FH wood screws. Make sure the back edge of the ramp is flush and aligned with the back of the base.

Then cut the stop to size and glue it to the ramp about 2 inches from the end. You can use a couple of screws to hold the stop in place while the glue dries, since you won't be sawing through this piece. Make sure that the stop is square (perpendicular) with the front edge of the ramp. After the glue is dry chip any excess from the chamfer groove between the base and ramp and the ramp and stop.

To use a shooting board to square up the

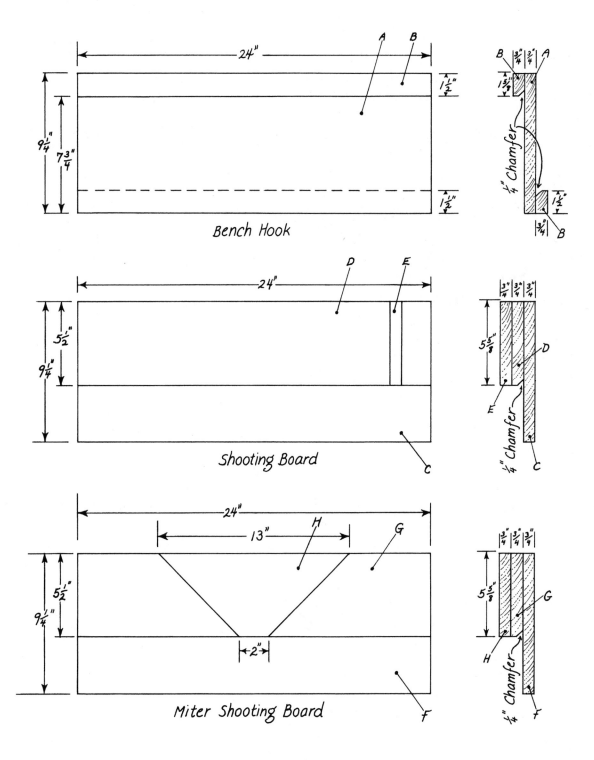

Bench Hook

Shooting Board

Miter Shooting Board

edge of a board, place the piece of wood on the ramp with its end against the stop and the edge you want to plane facing you. Then put your bench plane on its side with its sole facing the wood. Hold the board against the stop and parallel to the ramp and push the plane along the base. The plane is held at right angles to the board, allowing you to accurately dress up the edge. Plane away all saw marks and any wood above the layout line.

How to Build a Miter Shooting Board

The miter shooting board works on the same principle as the shooting board, only it holds the work at a 45-degree angle to the ramp. This tool is only as accurate as you make it, so work carefully. If you have a good miter box you can do it by hand. Otherwise take the piece of wood to the shop of a friend who has a table saw and cut the 45-degree angles there.

Glue and screw the ramp to the base as you would in making the shooting board. Don't forget to make the chamfer on the lower edge

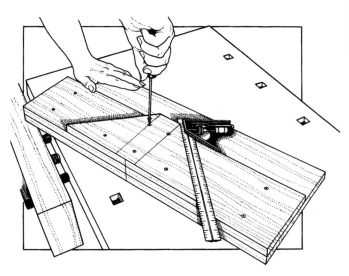

Use a combination square to accurately position the fence of the miter shooting board. Both faces must be exactly 45 degrees to the ramp and base to produce accurate work.

of the ramp. Then with 1¼-inch #6 FH wood screws, glue and screw the miter block to the center of the ramp. Check its alignment with the back edge of the ramp and to see that both of the edges are at a 45-degree angle to the front edge of the ramp.

This tool is used just like the shooting board, only the pieces are pushed against the face of the miter block at a 45-degree angle while you plane the end smooth and square.

TOOLS

Measuring tape	Crosscut saw
Combination square	Miter box
Hammer	Hand drill and bits
Screwdriver	Bench plane

PARTS LIST

Bench Hook

	Part	Number	Size	Material
A	base	1	¾″ × 9¼″ × 24″	birch
B	fence	2	¾″ × 1½″ × 24″	birch

Shooting Board

	Part	Number	Size	Material
C	base	1	¾″ × 9¼″ × 24″	birch
D	ramp	1	¾″ × 5½″ × 24″	birch
E	stop	1	¾″ × ¾″ × 5½″	birch

Miter Shooting Board

	Part	Number	Size	Material
F	base	1	¾″ × 9¼″ × 24″	birch
G	ramp	1	¾″ × 5½″ × 24″	birch
H	miter block	1	¾″ × 5½″ × 13″	birch

MATERIALS LIST

Material	Amount	Size	Used For
1″ × 12″ board	1	14 foot	base/fence/ramp
#6 FH (flat head) wood screws	12	1¼″	
carpenter's glue	1 small bottle		

·Stackable Sawhorse·

They're not pretty, but they are practical, and because of that you'll use these sawhorses in a variety of ways. They offer portable surfaces for working on projects around the house. Use them to support a door you're painting or to hold an old window you're working on. Topped with a ¾-inch sheet of plywood they become a sturdy work surface for fine woodworking.

With an I-beam backbone formed by one-by-fours nailed to the top and bottom of the two-by-four, the design is very strong. You can replace the top one-by-four with a new one when it becomes worn and pockmarked with saw cuts after a few years of hard use.

How to Build It

Building these sawhorses is very easy because you don't have to make any angled cuts to form the legs. The Parts List includes the parts necessary to build one set of sawhorses. Cut the backbone from the two-by-four lumber and cut the top and bottom rails from the one-by-four. Then cut the legs from the remaining one-by-four lumber.

Assembling the sawhorse is straightforward. Glue and nail the bottom rail to the two-by-four backbone. Don't apply glue to attach the top rail to the backbone; you want to be able to remove it later if it gets badly cut up. Use 2-inch all-purpose screws and carpenter's glue or 8d common nails and any type of construction adhesive. Allow the glue or adhesive to set up before you install the legs.

The legs are screwed to the sides of the two-by-four backbone and the edge of the bottom rail. To prevent the ends of the legs from splitting, drill ⅛-inch pilot holes for the screws. Use three 2-inch all-purpose screws per joint. Place the top row of screws about 1 inch down

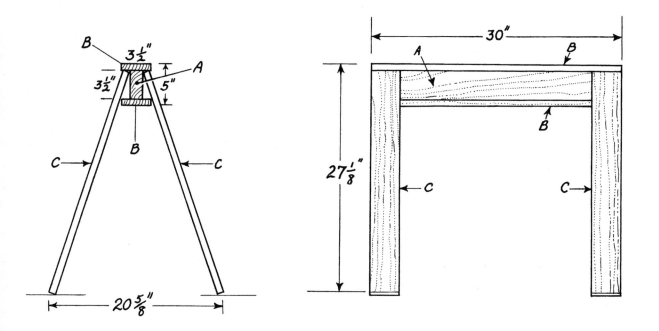

Use all-purpose screws to attach the sawhorse legs to the top of the backbone and edge of the bottom rail.

from the tops of the legs. Don't worry about the angle of the screws in the legs because they are long enough to penetrate deep into the backbone even when driven in perpendicular to the legs.

After the upper screws are installed, drill pilot holes through the legs for the lower set of three 2-inch all-purpose screws that hold the legs to the bottom rail. Use a try square to transfer the location of the center of the bottom rail to the legs. These screws should be angled so they go into the center of the edge of the bottom rail. They must be driven perpendicular to the edge of the rail or they may protrude from the board or split the wood. Install the legs on one side of the horse, then flip the unit and install the legs on the other side.

TOOLS

Measuring tape	Crosscut saw
Try square	Drill
Hammer	Screwdriver

PARTS LIST

	Part	Number	Size	Material
A	backbone	1	$1\frac{1}{2}'' \times 3\frac{1}{2}'' \times 30''$	pine
B	top/bottom rail	2	$\frac{3}{4}'' \times 3\frac{1}{2}'' \times 30''$	pine
C	legs	4	$\frac{3}{4}'' \times 3\frac{1}{2}'' \times 28''$	pine

MATERIALS LIST

Material	Amount	Size	Used For
2″ × 4″ pine	1	6 foot	backbone
1″ × 4″ pine	3	12 foot	rails/legs
2″ all-purpose screws	1 box		
carpenter's glue	1 small bottle		

·Glossary·

actual size   the measurement of something as it exists

aluminum nail   a nail made from an aluminum alloy; these nails are lightweight and will not rust

anchor   a type of fastener used to secure something to a wall

angle-cut   to cut a piece of wood at an angle

baseboard   decorative wood trim that conceals the joint between a wall and floor

bead   a thin application of glue or adhesive; a strip of wood with one edge molded in a decorative pattern

bench hook   a piece of flat wood placed on a workbench to protect the bench top from scarring

bevel   any joint between two surfaces that does not form a 90-degree angle; the edge of a board is cut at such an angle (usually 45 degrees) with a plane or chisel

bore   to make a hole in or through wood with a drill

butt joint   a plain square joint between two pieces of wood that meet end to end

centerline   a line drawn on the center of a piece of wood, used as a guide from which to measure and cut the piece accurately

chamfer   the beveled edge formed at right-angle corners of two pieces of wood

clamp   to hold two glued pieces of wood together while the glue dries

contour   carve, plane, or cut the face or outline of a shape on wood

crown   a type of molding, often intricately shaped, used at the joint between a wall and ceiling

cutout a design cut out of wood, or leftover wood cut out from a shape

dimensional lumber lumber in standard sizes

dowel a round length of wood that is sold in various diameters

doweled joint two pieces of wood joined together using a dowel as a pin that secures them

doweling jig a guide for making dowel holes

face the wider surface of a piece of wood; usually its most attractive side, which is the front

fence a wood or metal guide clamped to a table saw or work piece in order to guide the saw

finish nail a slender nail with a small head that does not protrude out of the wood's surface

flush refers to two or more pieces of wood aligned together so the surfaces are even and form a continuous plane

furring a thin strip of wood

galvanized nail a nail that has been treated to prevent rusting

grid pattern a framework of parallel and perpendicular lines used to copy a shape onto wood

hardwood wood that is dense and difficult to cut, such as oak or maple

jig (with guideholes) a device used as a guide for a tool or as a template

kerf the slot left by a saw as it cuts through a board; also a notch or groove cut into a board to make it more flexible

knot a variation in wood grain that is hard and looks like a blemish

laminate to build up layers of wood with glue forming an interesting cross section of end grain when it is cut

lattice narrow pieces of pine ¼ inch thick and approximately 1½ inches wide

layout lines marks showing how and where pieces of a woodworking project go together

miter cut a cut made at an angle for joining two pieces of board so that they meet at an angle

mortise a socketlike joint in the end of a piece of wood that is used to hold a tenon, or a projecting part, cut on another piece of wood

nominal size the dimensions of lumber after sawing but before it is planed

parting stop a small wood piece used in double-hung windows

peghole a hole in wood the right size for a peg

perimeter the combined lengths of all the sides of a space or project

pilot hole a preliminary small guidehole drilled into a board to guide a screw or nail and prevent the wood from splitting

plow to cut a groove in wood

plug a small wooden peg used to fill a hole in wood

rabbet   a groove cut in the surface or along the edge of a board to receive another board similarly cut

radius   the distance from the center of a circle to its perimeter

rail   a horizontal piece of wood within a frame structure, used in cabinetry and for windows

rip   to cut a board lengthwise

roofing nail   a nail with an extra-large head

scrap   a piece of wood used to hold pieces of a project together or to protect wood from the blows of a tool

screen bead   thin molding used to hold screening fabric in place

screen stock   a type of wood used to make screen windows and doors

scribe   to cut the edge or score wood with a sharp tool

shim   to adjust or make level by using a thin piece of wood to fill a space between two adjoining surfaces

shooting board   a frame to hold a board steady while it is being planed

softwood   wood such as pine that is soft to the touch and easy to nail into

square cut   to cut a board with straight ends

square up   to make a cut accurate so that two joining boards meet at a 90-degree angle

stile   a vertical piece of wood within a frame structure, used in cabinetry and for windows

stock   commonly used and available pieces of wood

tack   to fasten wood pieces together loosely

template   a pattern to follow for cutting out pieces of a project

tenon   a projecting part on the end of a piece of wood that fits into a corresponding hole (the mortise) in another piece to make a joint

trim out   to install molding and woodwork on walls

true up   to check that the edge or end of a cut board is square

wainscoting   vertical strips of wood or paneling installed on the lower part of a wall

waste side   the cut-off part of wood that is discarded

work   the piece of wood being worked on